Teaching Reading Strategies
With Literature That Matters to Middle Schoolers

Nancy Fordham and Alexa Sandmann

NEW YORK • TORONTO • LONDON • AUCKLAND • SYDNEY
MEXICO CITY • NEW DELHI • HONG KONG • BUENOS AIRES

To the many educators who daily pledge themselves to middle graders and literacy.
— Nancy Fordham

To Jack, whose steadfast friendship sustained me through trying times.
—Alexa Sandmann

Photo Credits

page 6: Time & Life Pictures/Getty Images; page 11: Sequel Creative/SODA; page 31: *The Blade*/Allan Detrich; page 35: Sequel Creative/SODA; page 50 (left): The Art Archive/Culver Pictures; page 50 (right): Library of Congress; page 55: Tom Hurst via SODA; page 70 (left): Library of Congress; page 70 (right): Heinrich Hoffmann/George Eastman House/Getty Images; page 77: Sequel Creative/SODA; page 97: Sequel Creative/SODA; page 115: AP Photos/Steven Senne; page 117: Sequel Creative/SODA

Cover design by Maria Lilja
Interior design by Melinda Belter

ISBN-13 978-0-439-46590-8
ISBN-10 0-439-46590-7

Contents

Introduction 5

Background 6

Reflection 7

About This Book 8

Closing Thoughts 9

Chapter 1
Forging One's Identity 11

The Janitor's Boy 12

The Well 15

Esperanza Rising 18

Through My Eyes 21

This Land Is My Land 26

Reproducible Pages 29

Chapter 2
Friendship 35

Pink and Say 36

Taking Sides 38

The Maze 41

Because of Winn-Dixie 44

Maniac Magee 46

Reproducible Pages 50

Chapter 3
Making Choices 55

The Butterfly 56

Speed of Light 59

Shiloh 62

The Graduation of Jake Moon 65

Surviving the Applewhites 67

Reproducible Pages 70

Chapter 4

Taking Action 77

The Children's Book of Heroes 78

Captain Kate 80

Hoot 83

Flying Solo 87

Burning Up 90

Reproducible Pages 94

Chapter 5

Immigration 97

Who Belongs Here? 98

When Jessie Came Across the Sea 100

The Orphan of Ellis Island 103

In the Year of the Boar and Jackie Robinson 106

The Circuit: Stories From the Life of a Migrant Child 110

Reproducible Pages 114

Chapter 6

The Pioneering Spirit 117

A Burst of Firsts: Doers, Shakers, and Record Breakers 118

Journey to Nowhere 121

The Journal of Augustus Pelletier:
The Lewis and Clark Expedition, 1804 125

The Breadwinner 128

Stargirl 131

Reproducible Pages 134

Appendix 141

Language Arts Standards 141

Social Studies Standards 142

References 143

Introduction

Among students of all grade levels, middle schoolers are the ones most keenly experiencing the angst of sudden, often explosive, growth. In an increasingly complex world, these "hormones on feet," as they have been wryly called, sometimes grapple with problems that confound even adults. We have learned through our combined years of teaching and raising young adolescents that they are understandably reluctant to discuss personal tribulations in large group settings. However, when motivated, they will animatedly sound off on issues involving third parties. Quality literature offers middle schoolers a way to safely step outside themselves long enough to gain a little perspective on life's challenges. Reading about others' misfortunes and missteps, as well as victories, and reflecting on them in meaningful ways encourages reason and resilience at a time when a strong sense of self is often still developing.

Effectively teaching middle school students requires using instructional practices tailored to their unique stage of development, which honors one of the 14 characteristics that the National Middle School Association (2003) considers essential to a developmentally responsive middle school. The lessons contained in this book also address other characteristics, such as creating a "challenging and integrative" curriculum (NMSA, p. 7). The variety of suggested books provides various points of entry into adolescent-friendly topics. Further, "multiple learning and teaching approaches" (NMSA, p. 7) are nurtured through the diverse suggestions for exploring each of the texts.

We believe the following are key ingredients for motivating and enhancing learning in middle school:

- Students need to **feel connected** to the academic material they are studying, and it is our job as teachers to forge that connection (Guthrie, 2004; Smith & Wilhelm, 2006).

- They learn best when the material matters and makes sense to them. Integrating content across subject areas (when possible) mimics real-life learning, lending **authenticity** and reinforcing important concepts from each discipline (Goodman, 1986; NMSA, 2003).

- Students need **guidance at all phases** of the reading process: before, during, and after (Duke & Pearson, 2002; Vacca & Vacca, 2005).

- Wisely selected and well-implemented **instructional strategies**, especially writing ones, support both reading and cognitive growth (Alvermann & Phelps, 2005; Atwell, 1998; Calkins, 1994; Duke & Pearson, 2002; Irwin, 1998; Vacca & Vacca, 2005).

- Students need and deserve a variety of reading materials written at **different levels**, as well as some **choice** in how they demonstrate understanding of those materials (Allington, 2002; Gunning, 2003; Tomlinson, 2003).

- There is no more important time than the middle years to provide instruction that helps students **develop empathy**, cultural sensitivity, and healthy values (NMSA, 2003; Trelease, 2001; Wormeli, 2003).

- Middle schoolers require **social interaction**, not just at lunch or recess, but in the classroom as well (Hidi & Harackiewicz, 2000; NMSA, 2003; Vygotsky, 1962, 1978; Wilhelm & Smith, 2006).

Recent research studies on factors that motivate adolescent literacy have produced consistent results: To be engaged, students must

- Connect personally to the material
- Feel competent and be given some choice
- Have teachers who help them develop the skills and strategies they need
- See reading and writing as integral to addressing a real problem or contributing to an authentic ongoing conversation
- Participate in meaningful contexts for learning
  (Guthrie, 2004; Wilhelm & Smith, 2006)

In the following two sections, co-author Nancy Fordham recalls planning a unit on Romeo and Juliet *for an all-male ninth-grade English class some years ago and then reflects on the process, paving the way for the approach offered in this book.*

Background

Making reading matter to ninth graders is rarely an easy feat, but when dealing with "antiquated" texts like Shakespeare, it's trickier yet. Work of mouth, then, about *Romeo and Juliet* was decidedly negative before we began this challenging play, and I wondered how I might overcome the bad press, on top of my students' general reluctance to read. How could I make Shakespeare relevant to students in 1994? Coincidentally, it was the same year that Jeff Harding's pre-Olympic assault on his wife Tonya's fellow skater and competitor Nancy Kerrigan gained international attention. *Time* magazine had published an issue with the bizarre attack as its feature article. The cover depicted a graceful, smiling Kerrigan mid-jump on the ice, a dark impression of Harding's face in the background. The words "The Star-Crossed Olympics" were displayed prominently. *Hmmm*, I thought, *"star-crossed" was the phrase Shakespeare himself used to describe Romeo and Juliet*. I decided to try making a connection between the unlucky pair and the Kerrigan-Harding incident, which every student knew about and was eager to discuss.

The next week, **before reading**, *Time* in hand, I showed the cover to my students, allowing them to survey and comment on it, which, as expected, they did without hesitation. Comments ranged from Kerrigan's looks to the mindset of an athlete who would go to such extremes to eliminate the competition. Finally, someone inquired about the phrase "star-crossed": What, exactly, did it mean? We launched into a discussion about the term and once they understood its connotation, they suggested other people and events they deemed ill-fated: the Donner Party, Amelia Earhart, the *Titanic*, the *Edmund Fitzgerald*, and so on.

Time, February 21, 1994

Then I told them the story of Evangeline, the mythic heroine of Longfellow's epic poem about two lovers separated during the Acadian expulsion from Nova Scotia in 1755. After a relentless search that took years, Evangeline finally located her beloved Gabriel who, as fate would have it, died in her arms. She herself died shortly thereafter.

Following the tale, one student suggested that it reminded him of the story of *Romeo and Juliet*, which he hadn't read but believed had a similar theme. This was the segue I'd hoped for! Acknowledging the accuracy of his observation and mindful of the adolescent concerns that so frequently occupied most of them, I introduced the play with a question: "Have any of you ever liked a girl your parents disapproved of?" Hands shot up. A few brave souls unabashedly volunteered anecdotes about family tensions that erupted amid such budding romances. Others, more reticent, nodded in recognition. Some, I knew, had never experienced this kind of discord. Yet, even at 14 and 15, every student could relate, and their interest was piqued.

Once they felt some connection to the characters, I was able to generate more anticipation by keying in on other story elements intriguing to adolescents—family feuds and romantic rivals, for instance. What typically happens when two families are feuding and two males are competing for the same woman? Why, fights, of course! And so it went. Without giving away the story, I helped my students see links between their own lives and those of the characters in the play. Doing all this required a significant chunk of my 50-minute English period. I could have lamented the "lost teaching time," but, I was convinced that the effort I'd devoted to helping students prepare for reading the play was time well spent. They were engaged and curious.

During reading, Shakespeare's Elizabethan English was a barrier, so I chose to use an audio recording as students followed along in their books. We stopped regularly to discuss the characters and plot, and we occasionally dramatized key scenes.

After reading, I gave students a choice of responses that would demonstrate their understanding of the play, none of which involved a test. Some students sketched or sculpted renderings of important scenes and wrote about their significance. Others elected to rewrite scenes in contemporary English and re-enact them. Still others chose a more traditional form of response: an essay focusing on prescribed aspects of *Romeo and Juliet.*

Reflection

All in all, I was pleased with my students' engagement with the play and their willingness to tolerate the difficult language. I believe they learned a great deal and even enjoyed it at times. However, hindsight and a growing understanding of the reading process tell me there was still more I could have done. While I would give myself high marks for building their background knowledge, helping them make connections, predict, and visualize plot elements, and for differentiating the assessments by allowing them a choice of authentic, performance-based tasks, I did not offer enough support during reading. Sure, we used a dramatic recording and discussed the play, which certainly helped. But I could have supported my struggling readers (and I had several) even more. I could have secured and encouraged the use of versions written in contemporary English. I could have read aloud portions of the play, modeling how I predicted, made connections with the story, drew inferences, and summarized. I could have used anticipation guides before students read certain scenes, or graphic organizers that would have helped them clarify character and plot elements. And I could have orchestrated purposeful small-group activities that encouraged both social interaction and learning.

"One of the defining characteristics of accomplished teachers is their willingness to regularly analyze, evaluate, reflect on, and strengthen the effectiveness and quality of their practice . . . to extend their knowledge, perfect their teaching, and refine their evolving philosophy of education."
(National Board for Professional Teaching Standards, 2001, p. 51)

I know better now. Though I currently teach university students, I still interact with middle school students and their teachers. No matter what the content, I encourage teachers to carefully prepare students for reading by building interest, motivation, and background knowledge. And I prod them to give students as many choices as possible for demonstrating their understanding of important concepts. I also encourage teachers to be much more attentive to the during-reading phase of comprehension, not leaving students on their own to struggle with the challenges many texts present.

We teachers, whatever our subject areas, need to scaffold students' comprehension as they read. That can best be done by showing students how we make sense of texts as we read, as well as by using a repertoire of proven instructional strategies that promote comprehension.

About This Book

Reading comprehension strategies are embedded in each chapter, with every selection. In many cases, we've provided explicit instructions for modeling a particular reading strategy. The reproducibles accompanying many of these strategies will help you implement them.

We have selected literature for this book that correlates with themes appropriate for middle school and commonly found in the language arts/social studies curriculum: forging one's identity; friendship; making choices; taking action; immigration; and the pioneering spirit. Moreover, the literature spans a variety of genres and reading levels—a must for developing students' comprehension skills. You may choose to focus on just one book in each chapter, or on several. Another option is to use several theme-related books for reading in literature circles. There is so much wonderful literature on the market today that can be used to enliven content in every discipline. High-quality trade books, whether fiction or nonfiction, are interesting, informative, and written at a variety of reading levels. Even poetry and picture books are appropriate. Many of them teach concepts similar to those in textbooks, which are often intimidating to students.

"The picture book format is . . . an elastic one, that has, particularly recently, been adapted for students of all ages and in various ways. Picture books encompass a wide range of subject matter. They can be used to enhance instruction in every content area . . . scaffold student understanding of a range of topics through formats that intrigue rather than intimidate . . . [and] can be a particularly rich resource for struggling readers and English language learners."
(Vacca & Vacca, 2005, pp.169–170)

We've also crafted this book with a teacher's time in mind. You will notice as you thumb through its pages that the lessons supporting each of the 30 books adhere to our belief in the importance of the three-part instructional framework: before-, during-, and after-reading strategies (Vacca & Vacca, 2005). You may wonder how lessons this comprehensive could possibly save you time. Well, here's the secret: *integration.* When you integrate interdisciplinary content with reading strategies, you actually free up valuable time. You are able to address important content standards and curricular topics while teaching essential skills.

We have taken a thematic approach to instruction, integrating two primary content areas: reading/language arts and social studies. For your convenience, we've identified under each book description the IRA/NCTE standards it addresses. In 1996, the International Reading Association and the National Council of Teachers of English published a joint set of Standards for the English Language Arts. While written as a set of 12 statements, they are intertwined—and not meant to be taught or learned separately. All are addressed within the choice of texts and variety of activities found in this book. In addition, we have included the Social Studies curriculum standards articulated in *Expectations of Excellence* (National Council for the Social Studies, 1994) that apply to each lesson. You will find both sets of standards in the Appendix, on pages 141 and 142.

The lessons are designed with current research about learning in mind. Activating and building background knowledge is a crucial first step that engenders intellectual engagement and emotional connection. Without these, students won't care about what you're trying to teach. That's why, in this book, you'll see considerable effort expended on before-reading strategies. While you may opt to omit some of the activities for each selected reading, try to complete at least one as a way to engage students.

"Big picture" concepts are the focus of both the during- and after-reading strategies. Ironically, the during-reading component of the reading process, where most students stumble, typically receives the least focused attention from teachers. Though simple written pieces require minimal teacher support and guidance, texts that challenge readers with complex ideas and vocabulary—or pieces in which you suspect students may miss some of the subtleties—mandate more teacher support *while* students read. Assigning a chapter or section for homework, followed by the traditional question/discussion format, is not always sufficient—nor motivating. (Note: Make it a point to observe how many students are actually engaged during these discussions!) Therefore, in this book, extended lists of questions are not suggested. Our hope is that students come to appreciate the "whole" of literature, the reason "real" readers, not "school-time readers," read text.

Allotting time to engage in after-reading strategies helps students debrief and refine their understanding of key concepts. Encourage students to question, consider, discuss, write, illustrate, dramatize, or otherwise expand on ideas gleaned through reading. Their content knowledge *and* literacy skills are then enhanced—a boon to students' intellectual and academic growth.

While the activities recommended in this book are text specific, the strategies can be adapted across texts. The most adaptable of reading strategies are activating background knowledge, predicting, and previewing, and we consistently recommend that you encourage students to use these.

From an instructional standpoint, reading aloud a particular chapter or part of a chapter typically enhances students' enjoyment and understanding.

If engagement with a required text or topic seems unlikely, an anticipation guide may be just the way to pull students into the ideas. You may also find that having students complete a K-W-L grid or stimulating interest with photos or realia may work just as well.

If summarizing is the goal, a story pyramid might help students create a competent final project as they play with words in order to fill out the organizer. You may also choose to try a discussion web.

If extending students' understandings is the goal, an I-chart may be a perfect research tool, or perhaps a compare/contrast chart or a writing frame.

While we have organized the strategies around a "before, during, and after" structure, these labels are not meant to be constrictive. You are the one who best knows your students and materials, and are the best-suited to determine the timing of the strategies and the emphasis placed on each.

> We don't recommend excessive disruption of students' reading—sometimes it's best to just let them go—however, wise teachers know when and how to increase instructional support during reading. Teacher modeling and the judicious use of a variety of instructional strategies help students see how proficient readers interact with text and assist them in extracting and organizing key ideas. Such strategies also increase the odds that students will be able to critically reflect on the information after reading.

Closing Thoughts

A key feature you'll notice as you use these lessons is that they incorporate a good bit of social learning—purposeful, but definitely social—where students must confer with one another to gather ideas and hear other perspectives. Middle schoolers need social interaction, and they can and do learn efficiently when it is properly structured. It takes time to teach students the social skills and work habits needed for group tasks. However, these are essential life skills, and you may be amazed at the levels of thinking students demonstrate in such contexts.

Like Kasten, Kristo, and McClure (2005), we believe in the power of literature to transform our students' lives. Many of the books in this text will touch students in ways that textbooks alone can never do. What an opportunity they present to discuss values and healthy, ethical decision-making! So, go ahead—try some of the literature and lessons that follow. We think you'll smile with satisfaction as you see your students enjoying literature, improving their literacy skills, expanding their content knowledge, and developing social understanding. While you are busy engaging your students' minds with these lessons, you will also be engaging something else that drives learning: their hearts.

Nancy Fordham
Alexa Sandmann

Forging One's Identity

Chapter 1

In this chapter, students will meet characters both fictional and real. Some characters simply face the everyday concerns of adolescence while others are thrust into problematic, sometimes painful circumstances. All emerge intact and wiser. These books help students get behind the eyes of men, women, and children with moral fiber— people with pluck, who confront tough issues like racism, poverty, and injustice. Students have the opportunity to examine the thinking processes behind characters' actions and consider alternatives that might have produced different results. They will learn that not all problems are easily solved, and choices made either deliberately or carelessly often carry profound consequences. If approached with a resolute spirit, however, hardships and losses can be borne, self-identity can be cultivated, and, ultimately, life can be celebrated—an important insight for adolescents.

The Janitor's Boy

by Andrew Clements

Kids at this developmental stage are beginning to separate from their parents. They are critically (and *critically* is the operative word here) more aware of, and place more importance on, what others think. This novel explores this issue in an environment students know well—a school. The insights into the changing relationship between the father and son are particularly well presented. Clements is never preachy, but nevertheless makes his message clear.

Because of burgeoning enrollment, the local school district builds a new junior high school. While it is being built, Jack's dad becomes the custodian of the temporary location, the "old high school." This is the central problem for fifth grader Jack, who attends this school. When no one knows that his dad is the custodian, everything is fine, but one day at school, his father, "John the Janitor," says, "Hi, son." Jack is angry and tries to get back at this dad. Over time, Jack refines his ability to define himself, both as his father's son and as an individual in his own right.

STANDARDS: IRA/NCTE Standards 1, 3, 4, 7, 11, and 12; NCSS Standards IV and V

MATERIALS

✔ Clements, A. (2000). *The Janitor's Boy.* New York: Simon & Schuster. (one per student)

✔ Story Pyramid (page 29, one per student)

✔ A variety of chewing gum, including watermelon-flavored bubble gum, enough for all students to sample and assess. (optional)

✔ Cunningham, A., & Young, M. Eds. (2002). *Guinness Book of Records.* New York: Bantam Books. (optional)

FEATURED READING COMPREHENSION STRATEGIES: Journal; Make Connections; Graphic Organizer: Story Pyramid

Before Reading

1. Ask students to respond to these questions as a journal entry:

   - *How hard would it be to have your father employed in the school you attend?*

   - *Would your comfort level change depending on his position there? What if he were a teacher? The principal? The custodian?*

   Invite students to share their perspectives, then collect all of the responses. After students finish reading the book, return them so they can reassess their perspectives.

2. The *New York Times Book Review* called *The Janitor's Boy* "a perfect book." Ask students to create a list delineating what makes a book "perfect."

3. If your school permits gum, divide the class into small groups and provide them with a variety of chewing gums, including watermelon-flavored bubble gum. Conduct a poll by asking students to determine which is "the smelliest." After reading, see if they came to the same conclusion as Jack does. Then, as a class, compile the results, and if time or inclination permits, graph the results. Again, ask students to compare their results with Jack's.

During Reading

1. In Chapter 13, Jack makes a list of ways he is *not* like his dad. At this point in students' reading, ask them to make a list of ways they are not like their dad (or another significant male in their lives), as well as ways they *are* like their dad. Girls could make a list of how they are *not* like their mom (or another significant female in their lives). Jack felt better once he had made the list. Discuss with students how they feel after making the lists.

MAKE CONNECTIONS

2. In Chapter 15, Jack believes he should suggest a new category of achievement to be included in the *Guinness Book of World Records*: "Greatest Quantity of Gum Removed From School Property During Four Hours." In small groups, ask students to imagine other categories that could be included. Then they can check to see if those categories already exist.

3. Before reading Chapter 18, ask students to write a paragraph defining panic. Read the chapter, and compare their scenarios of panic with Jack's.

After Reading

1. Once students have finished reading the novel, ask them to complete a Story Pyramid. The strategy works with any kind of fiction. Typically the longer the text, the more challenging this strategy is because of the variety of choices that can be made, including choosing which character is the central one. For this text, there would probably be little disagreement that Jack is the main character, but for other books, students may be able to make strong cases for more than one character. This kind of critical thinking is precisely what such strategies are all about!

On the first line, students should identify the main character. The next two lines should include two qualities or traits that character possesses. The third line has three spaces to describe the setting. Students can focus on place (in the woods) or time (300 years ago), or highlight various settings (woods, house, city), depending on the chosen text. The fourth line asks students to reveal the problem—in only four words. On lines five, six, and seven, using as many words as spaces, students summarize the main events of

Scholastic Teaching Resources: Teaching Reading Strategies With Literature That Matters to Middle Schoolers 29

Story Pyramid

_____
character

_____ _____
traits of character

_____ _____ _____
setting

_____ _____ _____ _____
problem

_____ _____ _____ _____ _____
first event

_____ _____ _____ _____ _____ _____
second event

_____ _____ _____ _____ _____ _____ _____
third event

_____ _____ _____ _____ _____ _____ _____ _____
resolution

SUMMARY:
_____
_____
_____

Adapted from: Macon, J., Bewell, D., & Vogt, M. E. (1991). *Responses to Literature*. Newark, DE: International Reading Association.

KEY BENEFIT
A Story Pyramid gives students the opportunity to review the story as a whole and write a "bare bones" summary.

the story, in chronological order. On line eight, in eight words, of course, they describe the resolution of the story in sentence form.

Completing the Story Pyramid works particularly well in groups—the strategy provokes great conversation as students justify decisions and word choice. Once students have completed their pyramids, ask them to write a summary paragraph.

2. Encourage students to review the criteria they created for "a perfect book." Discuss whether this book was perfect by their criteria. In what ways, if any, would they revise their criteria?

Extension Activities

- Jack has an extraordinary sense of smell. Ask students to prepare a short report on the sense of smell explaining why or how (or both) Jack might have this ability. Have them share their findings with the class.

- Invite students to research the history of gum, finding out how it is made, how much is chewed every year, and what the most popular brands might be and share their findings.

- Students can choose another of Clements' books to read, and then present a book talk to the class.

Further Reading

More books by Andrew Clements:
Frindle. (1998). New York: Simon & Schuster.
The Jacket. (2002). New York: Simon & Schuster.
The Landry News. (1997). New York: Simon & Schuster
The Last Holiday Concert. (2004). New York: Simon & Schuster.
Lunch Money. (2005). New York: Simon & Schuster.
The Report Card. (2004). New York: Scholastic.
School Story. (2001). New York: Simon & Schuster.
Things Not Seen. (2002). New York: Penguin Young Readers.
A Walk in the Woods. (2002). New York: Simon & Schuster.

For slightly shorter texts, try the books in the Jake Drake series:
Bully Buster. (2001). New York: Aladdin.
Class Clown. (2002). New York: Aladdin.
Know It All. (2001). New York: Aladdin.
Teacher's Pet. (2001). New York: Aladdin.

TECHNOLOGY LINKS
For information about author Andrew Clements on the Internet, visit these sites:
http://www.andrewclements.com
http://www.eduplace.com/kids/hmr/mtai/clements.html
http://www.edupaperback.org/showauth.cfm?authid=48
http://www.frindle.com

The Well

by Mildred Taylor

Readers familiar with Mildred Taylor's work will recognize the Logan family in this prequel to *The Land* and *Roll of Thunder, Hear My Cry*. Like her other novellas, *The Gold Cadillac*, *The Friendship*, and *Mississippi Bridge*, this short page-turner paints a compelling picture of human dignity in the face of racism.

Set in Mississippi in the early 20th century, the characters in *The Well* are so clearly drawn and the events so convincingly described that readers will bristle with indignance at the injustice the Logans are forced to tolerate. However, this story is more than a simplistic tale of good versus evil. Several of the main characters, including those in the Logan family, have flaws that escalate the conflict in the story. The events that emerge serve as an ideal vehicle for launching into a discussion about prejudice and conflict resolution.

Adolescents' passionate insistence on "fairness" combined with Taylor's superb story-telling talents will make it easy for teachers to ignite interest in this book. Deft teacher guidance will turn it into an excellent lesson in critical literacy.

STANDARDS: IRA/NCTE Standards 1, 2, 3, 7, 8, 9, 11, and 12; NCSS Standards I, II, IV, and VI

MATERIALS

✔ Taylor, M. (1995). *The Well.* New York: Scholastic. (one per student)

✔ Who's Who in *The Well* Tree Diagram (page 30, one per student)

✔ Dictionary

FEATURED READING COMPREHENSION STRATEGIES: Background Knowledge; Predict; Graphic Organizer: Tree Diagram; Morphemic Analysis

Before Reading

1. Ask students if family members have told stories about their childhoods. Encourage discussion, using this opportunity to emphasize literary genre. Explain that real-life experiences sometimes become books—appearing as nonfiction genres such as biography, autobiography or sometimes historical fiction, a genre that incorporates real and imagined events. *The Well*, we learn from Taylor's author's note on the story's origins, is historical fiction.

   BACKGROUND KNOWLEDGE

2. Call attention to this illuminating text feature by reading the author's note aloud and getting a discussion going with the following questions:

   • *Who is the author addressing?* (The reader.)

   • *What purpose does this author's note serve?* (Taylor wants to pass along important information: (1) The story evolved from family tales she heard as a child; (2) She believes they taught her a history about herself; and (3) The book's narrator is David Logan, the boy who is later the man and father in the book's sequel *Roll of Thunder, Hear My Cry.*)

PREDICT

3. Most editions of *The Well* have cover illustrations that invite examination and prediction. Establish a purpose for reading by encouraging students to scrutinize the cover. Invite students to predict characters, setting, and potential conflicts that may appear in the story.

KEY BENEFIT

A Who's Who diagram helps students distinguish among the characters and stay focused on the plot.

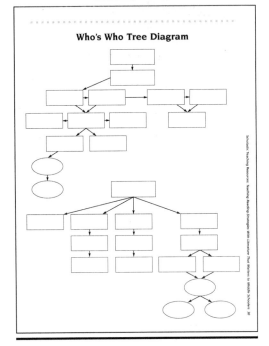

Who's Who Tree Diagram

Tip For more scaffolding, supply students with a partially completed graphic organizer that contains the various families' surnames. Software programs such as *Inspiration* make construction of these diagrams easy and fun for teachers and students.

During Reading

1. This compact narrative is populated with numerous characters and families who are integral to the plot. Reproduce and distribute the Who's Who in *The Well* Tree Diagram (Lannen, 1999).

2. Instruct students to add the characters' first names as they come across them while reading. Alternatively, you can position an oversize version of the organizer on a classroom wall or bulletin board where students can contribute illustrations, and justify their appropriateness.

3. Have students read and confer in small groups about the various characters' personality attributes and feelings, making notes as needed. To model, ask students to describe Hammer. List attributes on the board as students suggest them. "Quick-tempered" or "prideful" would be appropriate descriptors, for instance. Discuss the attributes as a class. Tell students to add these to their diagrams, next to Hammer's name. Students should then do the same for the other major characters.

4. Instruct students to use their diagrams and notes about the characters' attributes to describe how each character contributes to or defuses the conflict. If students need more support in making these associations, prompt them with statements and questions such as

* *Describe some occasions when Hammer's quick-temperedness made the situation worse.*

* *What might he have done instead?*

* *Who helped defuse the conflict? Why?*

After Reading

1. Once students understand the relationships between the characters, it is time to respond to the heart of the story: the prejudice and conflict that drive the action. The plot incidents are so provocative that students will be eager to discuss them. As they elaborate on events or actions they consider unjust, such as the whipping David and Hammer endure, list the events on the board.

2. Afterward, guide the class in thinking of a label that explains the reason these events occurred. Ask: *What word or words could explain the cause of these incidents?* (Prejudice). Scaffold students' thinking by asking questions such as these:

   - *Why did Charlie hate the Logans so much?*

   - *Why would Mr. Simms want to see David and Hammer whipped?*

   - *Can you think of a reason he would assume they were lying?*

   - *Why won't Mr. or Mrs. Logan confront Mr. Simms?*

3. After you have discussed prejudice as the impetus behind the action, model how to analyze the word's structure for meaning clues. Ask students if they recognize any of the word parts in *prejudice*. Most should readily be able to identify the prefix *pre-* (as in *prequel*), and some may notice the similarity between the root *judice* and *judge*. Next, ask them to hypothesize about the word's meaning. Then, have them find its definition in the dictionary. They can also trace its derivation from the Latin word *praejudicium*—prae (pre-) + judicium (judgment) or "previous judgment." Ask them to cite specific ways the definition applies to the story.

MORPHEMIC ANALYSIS

4. Finally, relate the story to the Author's Note you discussed before reading:

   - *Why did Taylor tell this story?*

   - *What might it have taught her about her history?*

   - *How might that have affected her?*

Extension Activities

- Encourage students to interview a family member and write his or her story. They should include an author's note that explains the story's origins.

- Locate newspaper and magazine articles that describe incidents of modern-day prejudice. Read them aloud or distribute them to small groups. As a class, identify the individuals or groups targeted, speculate about the reasons behind the treatment they receive, and relate those events to events in *The Well*.

- In the book, David's father and older brothers are often away from home "lumbering on the Natchez Trace." Direct students to use the Internet to learn about the trail and the economic opportunities its construction would have provided families like the Logans. Numerous sources including the National Park Service's Web site offer information on the history and geography of this famous trail, which stretches from Mississippi to Tennessee.

- Access American Memory, a Library of Congress Web site containing thousands of primary source documents to locate photos of sharecroppers and their homes. Share some with the class and generate a discussion about how the Simms family's status as sharecroppers might have affected their feelings toward the Logans.

Further Reading

More books by Mildred Taylor:

The Friendship. (1998). New York: Puffin Books.

The Gold Cadillac: A Fancy New Car and an Unforgettable Drive. (1998). New York: Puffin Books.

The Land. (2001). New York: Phyllis Fogelman Books.
Let the Circle Be Unbroken. (1991). New York: Puffin Books.
Mississippi Bridge. (1992). New York: Skylark.
The Road to Memphis. (1992). New York: Puffin Books.
Roll of Thunder, Hear My Cry. (1991). New York: Puffin Books.

TECHNOLOGY LINKS
For related information on the Internet, visit these sites:
   American Memory: http://memory.loc.gov
   The National Park Service: http://www.nps.gov/natt/index.htm

Esperanza Rising
by Pam Muñoz Ryan

Pam Muñoz Ryan's book captures the plight of migrant workers in the United States. Cited as an ALA Best Book and winner also of the Pura Belpré Award, given to a writer whose work best portrays the Latino cultural experience, this novel joins the author's growing list of quality books for children and young adults. Some high-interest story elements make this book a good choice for middle schoolers, who will be drawn to the "riches-to-rags" plot and the rich girl–poor boy friendship that develops between Esperanza and Miguel, the son of former family servants. However, there is a deeper social message to be examined here.

Esperanza Rising is inspired by the life of Ryan's grandmother, Esperanza Ortega, who, as a young girl, found herself propelled into a world far different from the one she had always known and taken for granted. In this fictionalized version, Esperanza is born into a privileged Mexican family. Her shining life comes to an abrupt halt, however, on the eve of her 13th birthday when bandits kill her father, and her unscrupulous uncles seize upon the occasion to profit for themselves. Left homeless and penniless, Esperanza and her mother escape with their devoted household servants to the United States, where they eke out a substandard existence as migrant workers. Engaging to read and reminiscent of *The Grapes of Wrath*, this story offers plentiful opportunities for exploring the lives of a group of people often disregarded in our society: those who harvest much of the food we eat.

STANDARDS: IRA/NCTE Standards 1, 2, 7, 8, 9, 10, 11, and 12; NCSS Standards I, II, IV, and VII

> **MATERIALS**
> ✔ Ryan, P. M. (2000). *Esperanza Rising.* New York: Scholastic. (one per student)
> ✔ Photo of a migrant worker (page 31, one per student)
> ✔ I-Chart (Inquiry Chart) (page 32, one per student)

FEATURED READING COMPREHENSION STRATEGIES: Background Knowledge;
Graphic Organizer: I-Chart (Inquiry Chart); Predict; Structural Analysis

Before Reading

1. Begin by displaying the photo of the migrant worker. Encourage students to examine the photo closely. Then initiate a discussion by asking these questions:

   - *Have you ever seen someone who looks like this? Where?*

   - *What can you tell about this person?*

2. Write responses on the board or chart paper. Facilitate thinking, if necessary, by suggesting students consider the following:

   - *Is the person a male or female? Child or adult?*

   - *Look closely at the worker's clothing. What is he/she wearing? Why?*

   - *Where is he or she?* (Look for a general location, such as "in a field" as well as hypotheses about a specific location, such as possible states, regions, and so on.)

   - *How large do you think this field is?*

   - *What is the worker's job?*

   - *What type of plants do you think these are?*

   - *Where do you think the worker has come from?*

   - *How do you suspect this person feels? What do you suppose he or she is thinking?*

Examine the photo closely. What do you suppose this person is thinking? Write your answer in the thought bubble.

3. Distribute copies of the photo to students. Tell them to fill in the thought bubble over the worker's head with what they believe he or she may be thinking. Have students share these with the class as an empathy-building exercise.

4. Tell students they will be reading a novel set in the 1930s about migrant workers from Mexico. Point out Mexico on a map if necessary. Ask students to share their perceptions of migrant workers. Record and discuss these impressions, considering their sources and validity.

5. Introduce the word *stereotype* and explain that learning more about people helps counter misconceptions and, thus, stereotyping. Elicit questions students may have about migrant workers, such as

   - *Where do migrant workers come from?*

   - *Where do they live when working?*

   - *How much do they earn?*

   Record questions and tell students they are going to conduct some research based on these.

I-Chart

Topic	Question 1 Where do migrant workers come from?	Question 2 Where do they live when they are working?	Question 3 How much money do they earn?	New Questions How have their living and working conditions improved since the 1930s?
Newspaper Source				
Internet Source				
Personal Interview				
Summaries				

Scholastic Teaching Resources: Teaching Reading Strategies With Literature That Matters to Middle Schoolers 32

KEY BENEFIT
An I-Chart, or Inquiry Chart, helps students organize their research. (Hoffman, 1992)

6. Distribute copies of the I-Chart. Students should select at least three questions that interest them and write those in the spaces provided at the top of the chart. (See example at left.)

Encourage them to suggest sources for finding answers to their questions (newspapers, the Internet, magazines, personal interviews, U.S. Department of Labor, social service agencies, and so on). They should list potential data sources in the spaces provided in the chart's left column.

Provide access to reference materials. As students locate answers to their questions, they should record them in note form in the corresponding spaces on the I-Chart grid. Model this procedure, showing students how to add bibliographic information in the appropriate "source" square on their chart.

After students have recorded answers to their questions, tell them to write summary notes in the bottom row of each column. These notes can then serve as the foundation for full-fledged research reports. New questions that arise during the investigation should be recorded in the right column of the chart and addressed as appropriate. For example,

- *How have their living and working conditions improved since the 1930s?*

PREDICT

7. Introduce *Esperanza Rising* to students and ask them to predict what the title may mean. (Note: *Esperanza* means "hope," a fact that is revealed at the end of the book.)

During Reading

1. As students read, encourage them to use the knowledge they are acquiring through their research to speculate about the accuracy of the migrant experience described in the book. Revisit the issue of stereotypes. Draw students' attention to the conversation between Miguel and Esperanza that starts with "Esperanza, people here think that all Mexicans are alike," from the chapter entitled "Los Aguacates (Avocadoes)." Lead a discussion about this dialogue, focusing on the validity of Miguel's comments. Is he correct? If so, what might it take to counter these perceptions?

2. Discuss Isabel's wish to be Queen of the May, and the fairness of cultural perceptions regarding beauty.

STRUCTURAL ANALYSIS

3. Keep track of the Spanish words in the novel, such as *rapido*, *un fantasma*, and *burrito*. Examine words and word parts that bear similarities to familiar English words. Then discuss ways Mexican culture has influenced America.

After Reading

1. Have students consider why the author opted to forego traditional chapter numbers in favor of fruits and vegetables as titles, e.g., "Las Uvas (Grapes)," "Las Papayas."

2. Bring produce into the classroom. Invite students to find out how it gets from fields or orchards to the grocery store. As a class, construct a flow chart that illustrates the steps in this process, including the field workers' role.

3. Access the Migrant Workers' Children Web site, where students can read about migrant life through the eyes of three teenagers. Discuss these accounts and brainstorm ways schools and communities can be more sensitive to the needs of migrant students and their families.

Extension Activities

- Remind students that Abuelita has favorite sayings, such as "Wait a little while and the fruit will fall into your hands," which she regularly shares with Esperanza. Invite students to collect favorite sayings or words of wisdom from their own family. Ask for volunteers to share and, as a class, discuss how they reflect cultural values and beliefs.

- Invite a guest speaker with knowledge of the migrant experience into your class.

Further Reading

Hesse, K. (1999). *Out of the Dust.* New York: Scholastic.

Hobbs, W. (2006). *Crossing the Wire.* New York: HarperCollins.

Krull, K. (2003). *Harvesting Hope: The Story of Cesar Chavez.* San Diego: Harcourt Brace.

TECHNOLOGY LINK

Migrant Workers' Children: http://users.owt.com/rpeto/migrant/migrant.html

Through My Eyes

by Ruby Bridges

This book is an autobiographical account of the Civil Rights Movement from the perspective of Ruby Bridges. She made history at 6 years old when she integrated the William Frantz school in New Orleans. Despite the protests of the people of Louisiana, including the governor, the federal law that demanded integration was enforced. First grader Ruby spent much of the school year in the building alone with her teacher; eventually some children began to attend school again, but Ruby, in essence, was privately tutored for the entire year.

In this informational text Ruby, now an adult, provides not only a context for that dramatic event in her life, but also a photographic account of those times. Quotes from prominent magazines and newspapers, such as *The New York Times* and *Life*, are included, as well as an excerpt from John Steinbeck's *Travels With Charley*. A reprint of Norman Rockwell's *The Problem We All Live With*, depicting Ruby surrounded by four U.S. marshals—her daily escorts and guardians—is also included. *Through My Eyes* provides an evocative place with which to begin a conversation about culture and racism with students.

STANDARDS: IRA/NCTE Standards 1, 2, 3, 4, 5, 6, 7, 8, 9, 11, and 12; NCSS Standards I, II, IV, V, VI, and X

MATERIALS

✔ Bridges, R. (1999). *Through My Eyes.* New York: Scholastic. (one per student)

✔ Computers with Internet capability or at least one book of Norman Rockwell's art such as Tom Rockwell's *The Best of Norman Rockwell* (Courage Books, 2000).

✔ Index cards

✔ Table of Contents Think Sheet (page 33, one per student)

FEATURED READING COMPREHENSION STRATEGIES: Predict; Preview; Examine Text Features

Before Reading

1. Read aloud the letter from Harry Belafonte that begins this text. Ask students if they believe that Ruby was "called by her country to perform an act of profound bravery—to become the black child in an all-white school." Was Ruby courageous? He says she "moved the hearts and opened the minds of millions of people." Ask student to predict whether they will find her story "an inspiration." Record the class's prediction.

2. Encourage students to take a leisurely "picture walk" through the book as you talk about a particular photograph that moves you. Share your thoughts and feelings about it with the students, describing in great detail the aspects of the photograph that are particularly important to you.

   For example, if you choose the photograph of the angry protesters on page 17, you may highlight the hateful words on the signs, their faces distorted in anger, and the fact that most of the protesters seem to be teenage boys. Discuss why these young men seem to be so threatened by integration.

3. Invite students to peruse the book and then choose a different picture that they find particularly interesting. As a prewriting strategy, ask them to turn to a classmate and explain their choice, each taking a turn. Then, ask students to write down what they said, in either a poetic or prose form. Ask them to title their writing, "From My Heart." While students are writing, you can model for them and write as well. When all are finished, read aloud what they wrote. It is an excellent way to bring closure to this activity and to create interest in reading the text in its entirety.

4. If possible, have the class visit a computer lab so that everyone can view the Web site, <u>art.com</u>. Once there, students should type in "Rockwell" in the search box. After that, ask them to visit the "art gallery" and choose a painting that they find particularly touching. Have them write its name and the reason why they chose it on an index card. Then, create a graph by "stacking" the index cards (placing one above the other) on a bulletin board or chalkboard. See which illustration receives the most votes, or if there is no clear winner, see if there are common themes among the students' choices. Finally, after discussing the breadth of topics and

themes, ask students to compare their choice with the illustration included within the text, "The Problem We All Live With" (page 25). Ask students how it is similar to the illustrations students chose as their favorites. Then, ask them how this painting is different.

During Reading

EXAMINE TEXT FEATURES

1. Help students recognize the value of the information provided to the reader in the tan "bottom bars" on many of the book's pages. As students begin to read the book, draw their attention to the variety of information in those informational bars, such as excerpts from legal documents, quotes from Ruby's family and her teacher at the Frantz school, and statements from books, newspapers, and magazines. Ask students why such information was included in the book. Help them understand that this highlights the various sources of information that document this historical event—the power of multiple sources.

2. As students read, ask them to keep a list of significant events in Ruby's life.

After Reading

1. Students may notice that this text doesn't have a table of contents. Talk about the importance of having a table of contents and hypothesizing why this particular book does not.

   After the class comes to agreement that a table of contents is typically a handy tool to have as a reader, discuss how students could create one for this book. Lead students in an investigation into the book's structure. They'll find that there are no chapter labels, but that the book has been broken into sections with bold-face headings. Hand out the Think Sheet. As the directions state, after students have read the entire text, they can create a table of contents by first grouping the sections into chapters.

2. Once students have sectioned the text, ask them to provide chapter names for each chapter, not simply a number. This strategy is particularly helpful in nurturing their understandings of what constitutes a chapter—focus on one topic. Students may discover that they want to regroup sections. Encourage revision. It is the hallmark of an engaged learner. See the example at right for one possible set of chapter groupings and titles. This example is certainly not the only way the chapters could be arranged. If students can make a case that seems logical, accept their alternative groupings.

3. Finally, you may want to point out to students that the section "Preface to My Story" is set apart from the rest of the headings. Make sure students know what a preface is. Ultimately, the point of this activity is to nudge students' thinking about how writers conceptualize and organize information and why a table of contents is such a convenient tool for the reader.

Table of Contents Think Sheet

After reading *Through My Eyes*, create a table of contents, using all the section headings as listed below. First, create "chapters" by grouping the sections. Then name each chapter. Remember to choose a name that connects the sections in each group.

Preface to My Story 4

Chapter 1: Beginnings
Born in the Deep South 6

A New Home 8

One Year in an All-Black School 10

Chapter 2: Changes
My Mother Breaks the News 13

November 14, 1960 15

The First Day at William Frantz 18

Going Home 20

Chapter 3: Heartache
My First White Teacher 22

What a Passerby Wrote 24

Some Show Courage 26

Another First Grader 28

Three Little Girls at McDonogh 30

Riots in New Orleans 32

A Week of Trouble 34

Chapter 4: Hope
We Are Not Alone 36

More Support as I Go Back to School 38

Through the Winter With Mrs. Henry 40

I Draw Pictures for Dr. Coles 46

I Have Trouble Eating and Sleeping 48

The End of First Grade 50

Chapter 5: Reflections
Mrs. Henry Is Gone 52

Time Line 55

Let Me Bring You Up to Date 56

Scholastic Teaching Resources: *Teaching Reading Strategies With Literature That Matters to Middle Schoolers* 33

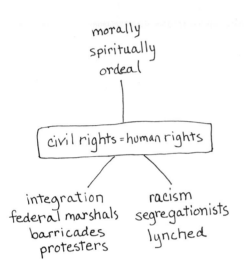

To make this understanding concrete, ask students several questions about the text for which they are not likely to recall the answers. For example, you may ask, *Who were the other children who were supposed to attend Frantz Elementary with Ruby?* Ask them to look in the book to find the answer. Then ask them if they can think of a faster way to find the information. Hopefully, they will realize that they can skim their table of contents to find the section most likely to contain the answer, in this case, Chapter 2, "Childhood Ends."

4. The timing of discussing vocabulary is always a challenge. Some educators believe that vocabulary should always be discussed before reading, others prefer to discuss the words when they present themselves in the reading, and still others believe that after reading the whole, particular words are best understood.

All of the critical vocabulary for *Through My Eyes* is, of course, related to the civil rights of Americans, particularly African Americans. Using the words civil rights as the center of a semantic map, challenge students to cluster the words in a way that helps them remember the definitions of each. The following is a list of words students can use in their semantic maps:

civil rights (Dear Reader)	barricades (p. 16)
human rights (Dear Reader)	protesters (p. 20)
racism (p. 4)	morally (p. 26)
integration (p. 4)	spiritually (p. 26)
segregationists (p. 4)	lynched (p. 36)
federal marshals (p. 14)	ordeal (p. 46)

Again, finding the one "right" way to cluster these words is not the point. However, a final semantic map may look like the one above.

Have students discuss their maps as a class. Students who clustered the words as they are listed in the example may say:

I put *morally, spiritually,* and *ordeal* together—and above *civil rights*—because civil rights are morally right. No human being is less than any other human being, no matter what skin color he or she might have. I put *spiritually* next to it because I believe that is what God believes, too. And I put *ordeal* there because Ruby's experience lasted nearly an entire school year. Her experience was an ordeal, a lo-o-o-ong experience.

I put *human rights* next to *civil rights* because I believe they are equal concepts. All Americans are entitled to be treated nicely, in a civil way.

Integration began a new cluster because that's what caused the *federal marshals*—like the president's policemen—to be called in. Because black and white children were supposed to attend the same school, *barricades* had to be put up around the school to keep the *protesters* from hurting Ruby. While the barricades did keep the protesters from physically touching Ruby, unfortunately, the barricades could not protect her from their ugly words, which came over the wooden fences all too clearly.

In the last circle are *racism*, *segregationists*, and *lynched* because segregationists believe in racism. They believe that some people should not mix with them because they are superior. In fact, these racists believe this so strongly that they were willing to defy the law and kill people or lynch them if they believe they are of an inferior kind.

5. Ask students to trade their list of "significant events" with a classmate and look for similarities and differences. Then as a class, have students choose the five most critical moments in Ruby's life and justify each choice.

Extension Activities

- Consult the Norman Rockwell Museum's Resource Packet for Educators for extensive activities related to the illustrations of Norman Rockwell: http://www.normanrockwellmuseum.org/educational/teacher_resource.pdf

- Invite a pair of students to go to the Online NewsHour Web site from PBS to find an interview with Ruby Bridges, download the interview, and, each taking a part, role-play this interview for classmates.

- Rent or purchase the film *Ruby Bridges* (1998), directed by Euzhan Palcy, a thoughtful movie that will remain in students' heads and hearts for years to come.

Further Reading

Marshall, H., Sorrentino, S., & Otto, C. (1998). *The Ruby Bridges Story*. The Wonderful World of Disney Series. New York: Little, Brown.
Coles, R. (2000). *The Story of Ruby Bridges*. New York: Scholastic.

TECHNOLOGY LINKS
Online NewsHour from PBS:
  http://www.pbs.org/newshour/bb/race_relations/jan-june97/bridges_2-18.html
For more information about civil rights, then and now, visit these sites:
  http://www.civilrightsproject.harvard.edu
Ruby's father won the Purple Heart. For its history, as well as information about why the purple heart is awarded, check out this site:
  http://www.purpleheart.org

This Land Is My Land

by George Littlechild

Acclaimed artist George Littlechild has produced a colorful picture book that, though simple in design and text, contains a moving message for middle schoolers about his life as a Plains Cree Indian. Students will be attracted to the book's vibrant illustrations, and you can be assured that you are sharing a book that has captured several awards, including the National Parenting Publications Award. Don't be deterred by the picture book format. This book's theme is anything but juvenile. The author demands through words and images that readers come to some mature realizations.

Using art therapeutically to express feelings of both pain and hope, Littlechild offers the reader a visual journey through the history of his people and his own family. "My goal," he says, "is to heighten awareness of the history and experiences of Native Peoples of the Americas and to promote understanding among all peoples." In the classroom his book serves as a gentle reminder about whom the Americas really belong to—*all* of us.

STANDARDS: IRA/NCTE Standards 1, 2, 4, 6, 8, 9, 11, and 12; NCSS Standards I, II, III, IV, and VI

MATERIALS

✔ Littlechild, G. (1993). *This Land Is My Land*. San Francisco: Children's Book Press. (one per student)

✔ CD: "This Land Is Your Land" (We prefer the version by Peter, Paul, and Mary.)

✔ CD player

✔ Song lyrics (available on the Internet)

✔ Map of North America

✔ Compare/Contrast Chart (page 34, one per student)

FEATURED READING COMPREHENSION STRATEGIES: Think, Pair, Share; Predict; Infer; Graphic Organizer: Compare/Contrast Chart

Before Reading

1. One powerful song from the turbulent 1960s is Peter, Paul, and Mary's version of the Woodie Guthrie song, "This Land Is Your Land." Your students may not be very familiar with this tune. Possibly they've heard it only at a Fourth of July celebration, for instance. It's time to acquaint your class with this classic! Before introducing Littlechild's book to students, ask them if they have ever heard the song, distribute the written lyrics, and then play it for them. (Remember to sing along!)

2. Be sure a large map of North America is visible. As the song plays softly in the background, help students locate the "New York islands, the redwood forests, and the Gulf Stream waters" on the map.

3. Next, instruct students to use the strategy Think, Pair, Share.

- First, students read the song's words and think about their meaning. Students should especially consider the line "This land was made for you and me."

- Ask them to make a list of the possibilities that come to mind when they consider the question, "Who are 'you and me'?" With a partner, they can share their thoughts.

- Discuss as a whole class the locations mentioned in the song.

4. On a transparency, chalkboard, or chart paper, record students' thoughts on whose land this is. Extend thinking and responses by prodding students to expand their list of "you and me,"—that is, every group or person they think this land belongs to.

5. When you have a reasonably inclusive list, ask students to consider how each group or individual came to be on this land. Encourage the observation that Native Americans were the first people to inhabit the Americas, and that the rest of us came later. See the Technology Links section for a list of Web sites with historical information about Native Americans.

6. Introduce George Littlechild's book to students. Examining the cover, talk about the title, the author, and his illustration. Encourage students to make predictions about the book's contents. On a map, locate the region occupied by the Plains Cree Indians of Canada.

KEY BENEFIT

Think, Pair, Share is a simple cooperative learning activity that holds individual students accountable for thinking and contributing, yet incorporates the social interaction adolescents crave and through which they are exposed to multiple perspectives. It's also a great way for English Language Learners to practice oral language skills in the security of a small group setting.

THINK, PAIR, SHARE

PREDICT

During Reading

1. Read the book aloud, discussing the text and illustrations. When finished, refer again to the book's illustrations, noting especially page 6, which depicts Littlechild's version of a Native American encountering Columbus for the first time. Ask:

- *What might the Native American be thinking?*

- *How would his view of life be different from those of the explorers?*

2. Reproduce and distribute the Compare/Contrast Chart to help students compare and contrast the beliefs of the people of the Cree Nation with those of the Europeans who conquered them.

3. As you read, guide students in completing the chart, rereading as necessary.

Compare/Contrast Chart

Beliefs about . . .	People of the Cree Nation	Europeans
Ancestors		
Animals		
Native culture		
Beauty		
Land		

INFER

After Reading

1. Reviewing the chart with a partner affords opportunities for talking about belief systems. Note that in some cases students will be required to make inferences about the beliefs to which the chart refers. You can help them by pointing out that actions are often evidence of beliefs.

2. Discuss students' responses as well as the term *culture*. Is it valid to value one culture above another? Conclude by asking students to consider again whose land this is, and whose it should be.

3. Littlechild's vivid artwork invites close examination. Ask students to discuss the illustration on page 21 depicting a Cree warrior sitting atop a red horse among a "sea of white horses." In the accompanying text, Littlechild describes the pain of being ridiculed for being "different." Finally, ask students to discuss and journal about how it feels to be an outsider.

Extension Activities

- Find news articles that focus on the circumstances or treatment of Native Americans today. How have conditions changed?

- Obtain a copy of Chief Seattle's famous speech on the settlers' treatment of Native Americans. Examine the document and discuss the views reflected in it.

- Have students investigate the Navajo Code Talkers and their critical role in World War II. Discuss the level of recognition they received by their country.

Further Reading

Bruchac, J. (2001). *The Journal of Jesse Smoke: Trail of Tears,* 1838. My Name Is America Series. New York: Scholastic.

Stein, R. C. (1993). *The Trail of Tears.* San Francisco: Children's Book Press.

TECHNOLOGY LINKS

A history of the Plains Cree people: http://www.schoolnet.ca/aboriginal/plains_Cree/
Navajo Code Talkers: http://www.history.navy.mil/faqs/faq61-1.htm

Story Pyramid

_____ character

_____ _____ traits of character

_____ _____ _____ setting

_____ _____ _____ _____ problem

_____ _____ _____ _____ _____ first event

_____ _____ _____ _____ _____ _____ second event

_____ _____ _____ _____ _____ _____ _____ third event

_____ _____ _____ _____ _____ _____ _____ _____ resolution

SUMMARY:

_____
_____
_____

Adapted from: Macon, J., Bewell, D., & Vogt, M. E. (1991). _Responses to Literature_. Newark, DE: International Reading Association.

Who's Who Tree Diagram

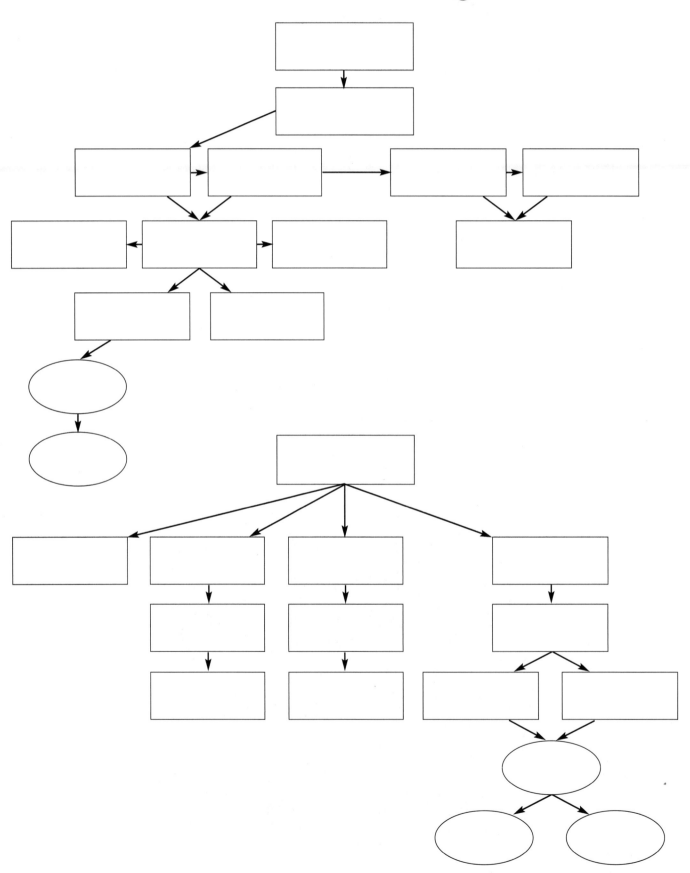

Examine the photo closely. What do you suppose this person is thinking?
Write your answer in the thought bubble.

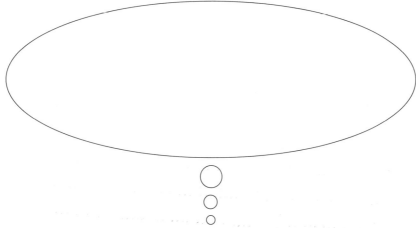

I-Chart

Topic	Question 1	Question 2	Question 3	New Questions
Newspaper Source				
Internet Source				
Personal Interview				
Summaries				

Table of Contents Think Sheet

After reading *Through My Eyes*, create a table of contents, using all the section headings as listed below. First, create "chapters" by grouping the sections. Then name each chapter. Remember to choose a name that connects the sections in each group.

Preface to My Story 4

Born in the Deep South 6

A New Home. 8

One Year in an All-Black School 10

My Mother Breaks the News 13

November 14, 1960 15

The First Day at William Frantz 18

Going Home 20

My First White Teacher 22

What a Passerby Wrote 24

Some Show Courage 26

Another First Grader. 28

Three Little Girls at McDonogh 30

Riots in New Orleans 32

A Week of Trouble 34

We Are Not Alone. 36

More Support as I Go Back to School. 38

Through the Winter With Mrs. Henry 40

I Draw Pictures for Dr. Coles 46

I Have Trouble Eating and Sleeping 48

The End of First Grade. 50

Mrs. Henry Is Gone. 52

Time Line 55

Let Me Bring You Up to Date 56

Compare/Contrast Chart

Beliefs about . . .	People of the Cree Nation	Europeans
Ancestors		
Animals		
Native culture		
Beauty		
Land		

Chapter 2

Friendship

Anyone familiar with middle schoolers is aware of the pivotal role friends play in their lives. This chapter helps young people expand their concept of friendship beyond the confines of same-age, same-background, same-interest peers. Through the literature presented, students will explore friendships between young and old, black and white, the gifted and the average, on so on. They will consider questions such as *What brings people together? What needs do friends fulfill? How do we define* friend*? Can people who are very different form strong friendships? Do we ever dismiss people as potential friends? Why? How is true friendship manifested?*

Pink and Say

by Patricia Polacco

Polacco, an acclaimed writer and illustrator, recounts the story of two unlikely friends in this touching tale. Deceptively straightforward in both its story and artwork, the book offers rich themes for middle schoolers to explore. Suitable for use with a study of the Civil War or any topic in which students examine issues of slavery, freedom, race relations, or our capacity for humanity and inhumanity. It makes an excellent Read Aloud. With significantly more text than the standard picture book, however, you may want to break the reading into two sections.

> **Tip** While this book can easily stand on its own, students will most appreciate *Pink and Say* if they first have some background knowledge about the Civil War.

As is the case with many of Polacco's books, *Pink and Say* is a true story, passed down through her family by her great-great-grandfather, Sheldon Russell Curtis, who is also the narrator. Set during the Civil War, it is the tale of two Union soldiers who meet by happenstance when Pinkus (nicknamed Pink), who is black, rescues the wounded Sheldon (Say), who is white. Pink takes Say to the ruined Georgia plantation where his mother, Moe Moe, is surviving alone, and she nurses Say back to health. Meanwhile, Pink and Say forge a deep friendship that is later marred by tragedy. Dedicated to Pinkus's memory, the story is unforgettable.

STANDARDS: IRA/NCTE Standards 1, 2, 3, 4, 5, 7, 8, 9, 11, and 12; NCSS Standards I, II, III, and IV

MATERIALS

✔ Polacco, P. (1994). *Pink and Say*. New York: Scholastic. (one per student)

✔ Photos of Union and Confederate soldiers (page 50)

✔ McKissack, P. & McKissack, F. (2002). *Christmas in the Big House, Christmas in the Quarters*. New York: Scholastic.

FEATURED READING COMPREHENSION STRATEGIES: Background Knowledge; Predict; Context Clues; Dramatize

Before Reading

BACKGROUND KNOWLEDGE

1. To build background knowledge, begin by displaying a photo or transparency of Civil War soldiers. Ask students to describe what they see. Be sure students note the soldiers' ages, as well as details about their uniforms. Explain that many soldiers were mere boys, as were Pink and Say.

2. Discuss the Union and Confederate political positions and refer students to a map where they can review the division between Northern and Southern states. Photos or diagrams of Southern plantations depicting the distinction between the "big house" and the slave quarters will also be useful to students in establishing the context for the brief visit Pink and Say pay to the remains of Master Aylee's house. Patricia and Frederick McKissack's book *Christmas in the Big House, Christmas in the Quarters* is a first-rate source for illustrations showing these contrasts.

3. Introduce *Pink and Say,* paying special attention to the cover illustration, which depicts the title **PREDICT** characters reading a book. Explain to students that the two are Civil War soldiers. Discuss their probable ages and set a purpose for listening by asking students to speculate about the plotline.

During Reading

1. Read aloud Polacco's foreword. Have students identify the narrator (Say) and ask them to revise their predictions about the plot based on the limited information.

2. As you continue to read the story, **CONTEXT** pause to elicit further comments **CLUES** and predictions and briefly discuss unfamiliar vocabulary words crucial to students' comprehension. (*Marauder* is one possibility. Be sure to point out context and visual clues that hint at the word's meaning.) Call attention to the author's frequent use of "hands" in the book's text and illustrations.

After Reading

1. Encourage students to **DRAMATIZE** share feelings and confirm or refute predictions about the story, then discuss the issues raised in it: the war, the friendship between Pink and Say, fear and bravery, the "sickness" (Pink's term for slavery).

2. This story is ideal for dramatization. Small groups of students can script and present reenactments of text segments. Have them add authenticity to their performances by researching topics relevant to their particular section of the story: the Southern plantation system, treatment of slaves and laws regarding them, Union and Confederate soldiers, Abraham Lincoln, and the prisoner of war camp (Camp Sumter) at Andersonville, Georgia. Narrators should provide a context for each performance by embedding the group's research findings in the reenactments.

3. Visit the Southern Poverty Law Center's <u>Teaching Tolerance</u> Web site to gather information about classroom lessons related to equity and justice.

4. Discuss the characteristics of friendship. Investigate examples of some famous interracial or intergenerational friendships such as that of Chicago Bears running back Brian Piccolo and his teammate Gale Sayers (show the movie *Brian's Song*) or sports columnist Mitch Albom and his college professor Morrie Schwartz (from the book *Tuesdays With Morrie*).

Confederate Soldier   Union Soldier

KEY BENEFIT
Primary sources—firsthand, "eyewitness" accounts and documents —are often fascinating and help students develop historical reasoning.
(Parker, 2001)

KEY BENEFIT
"Dramatic response activities lead toward the development of narrative competence, increased literary understanding, increased comprehension, oral language development, and the opportunity for empathetic emotional insight."
(Galda & West, 1996, p. 183)

Extension Activities

- Use the Internet to locate diary entries penned by prisoners at Andersonville. Read these primary sources in class and display them on a bulletin board. Supplement this research by showing one of two documentaries: *The Andersonville Diaries* or *Andersonville*. Both bring to life the horrific conditions prisoners endured in the notorious military prison—a revelatory experience for older middle schoolers.

- Have students research modern policies regarding prisoners of war.

Further Reading

Fleischman, P. (1993). *Bull Run*. New York: HarperTrophy.

Freedman, R. (1997). *Lincoln: A Photobiography*. New York: Clarion Books.

Murphy, J. (1990). *The Boys' War: Confederate and Union Soldiers Talk About the Civil War*. New York: Clarion Books.

TECHNOLOGY LINKS

American Memory: http://memory.loc.gov.

For information about Andersonville, or Camp Sumter as it was officially known, visit the National Park Service's Web site: http://www.nps.gov/ande/.

For ideas and resources for teaching about diversity and tolerance, visit the Teaching Tolerance Web site: http://tolerance.org.

Taking Sides

by Gary Soto

Taking sides is rarely a comfortable position to be in. Taking sides involves choosing one side or position rather than another. Middle schoolers are particularly sensitive about "choosing sides" because their sense of identity is so tightly connected with their peers—a classic dilemma explored in this contemporary novel.

Fourteen-year-old Lincoln Mendoza, a talented basketball player, feels compelled to make choices after he moves from his inner-city Hispanic neighborhood to a white suburban one. He does not like feeling torn between old friends and the new ones he wants to make. He does not like feeling guilty for being in the new neighborhood when he returns to visit friends in the old one. While basketball is important to this story, the meaning of friendship and how it is expressed is even more central.

Gary Soto is one of today's most celebrated writers, his books having sold more than a million copies. He began his writing career as a poet and has since written many novels for middle-grade students, as well as personal narratives about growing up in Fresno, California. In recent years, he has come out with picture books, as well as novels for both young adult and adult readers, and he continues to write poetry for readers of all ages. *New and Selected Poems* (1995) was nominated for the National Book Award, and he has received fellowships from the Guggenheim Foundation as well as the National Endowment for the Arts.

STANDARDS: IRA/NCTE Standards 1, 3, 4, 5, 9, 10, 11, and 12; NCSS Standards I, IV, and V

MATERIALS

✔ Soto, G. (1991). *Taking Sides*. San Diego: Harcourt Brace Jovanovich.

✔ Soto, G. (1991). *A Summer Life*. New York: Laurel-Leaf.

✔ Soto, G. (1992). *Living Up the Street*. New York: Laurel-Leaf.

✔ Soto, G. (2003). *Pacific Crossing*. San Diego: Harcourt Paperbacks.

✔ Soto, G. (1995). *Canto Familia*. San Diego: Harcourt.

✔ Soto, G. (2005). *Neighborhood Odes*. San Diego: Harcourt.

✔ Quick Summary Think Sheet (page 51, one per student)

FEATURED READING COMPREHENSION STRATEGIES: Quickwrite; Graphic Organizer: Venn Diagram; Summarize; Text-to-Text Connections

Before Reading

1. Ask students to do a "quickwrite" (Elbow, 1998). In this instance, give students five minutes to write a definition of *friendship*. Sharing is always an important part of a writing activity. Ask willing students to share their perspectives and then collect their responses so that students can reassess their perspectives after they finish reading the book.

> **QUICKWRITE**
>
> **KEY BENEFIT**
> A quickwrite helps students rapidly collect their thoughts on a particular topic.

2. As a class, have students create a definition of *loyalty*. Then complete a Venn diagram illustrating how the two concepts, friendship and loyalty, are similar and different.

> **VENN DIAGRAM**

During Reading

1. In Chapter 1, Soto relays that Lincoln "had moved from the Mission District of San Francisco, an urban barrio, to Sycamore, a pleasant suburban town with tree-lined streets" (p. 2). In the next four sentences, he repeats the phrase "tired of" and then concludes with eight concrete items to help the reader visualize why Lincoln's mother decided they would move. Ask students to write their own paragraph. They should follow a similar pattern, using the phrase "tired of," or one of their own choosing, repeating it three times at the beginning of sentences, and then ending the paragraph with concrete details that further their points. Other phrases students could choose are "excited about," "angry about," "interested in," "fascinated by," and "looking forward to."

2. Soto uses Spanish words throughout the novel. Discuss with students why he would choose to do so, helping students to understand that including them provides more authenticity to his text.

3. As students read, ask them to use the Quick Summary Think Sheet to provide each numbered chapter with a chapter title.

Quick Summary Think Sheet

After you read each chapter, write a title for it, summarizing the key idea.

Chapter 1 _____

Chapter 2 _____

Chapter 3 _____

Chapter 4 _____

Chapter 5 _____

Chapter 6 _____

Chapter 7 _____

Chapter 8 _____

Chapter 9 _____

Chapter 10 _____

Chapter 11 _____

Chapter 12 _____

Chapter 13 _____

Scholastic Teaching Resources: Teaching Reading Strategies With Literature That Matters to Middle Schoolers 51

After Reading

1. This book honors the challenges of life. Read aloud one of the personal narratives in Soto's *A Summer Life* or *Living Up the Street*. Discuss the narrative's features: Soto shares a story from his youth in which he makes a discovery about life. Ask students to do the same, to write about an event in their lives from which they learned something. If possible, it should be an experience they had with a friend.

2. Ask students to read the sequel *Pacific Crossing*. Then, ask them to think about what the central issue of a third book with Lincoln and Tony might be and then write the outline of that book.

TEXT-TO-TEXT CONNECTIONS

3. Read aloud any of Soto's poems in *Canto Familia* or *Neighborhood Odes*. Then ask students to celebrate the "ordinary" of their own communities by writing their own odes. Collect their poems as a class book.

Extension Activities

- Lincoln admires the Sphinx and the Nile in Egypt. Ask students to consider why he finds this monument and river so fascinating. Individuals or small groups can research these topics, along with others concerning Egypt that they find intriguing, and then present their findings to the class in a "news show" format.

- Monica's father requires her to take aikido. What kind of martial art is it? How does it compare with tae kwon do or jujitsu or others? As a class, create a chart with the type of martial art on the left-hand side and various characteristics across the top. Compare and contrast the various forms.

- Invite students to choose another of Soto's books to read and present a book talk.

Further Reading

Other works by Gary Soto:

POETRY

Fearless Fernie: Hanging Out With Fernie and Me. (2002). New York: Putnam.

A Fire in My Hands. (2006). San Diego: Harcourt.

Worlds Apart: Traveling With Fernie and Me. (2005). New York: Grosset & Dunlap.

NOVELS

Accidental Love. (2006). San Diego: Harcourt.

Boys at Work. (1995). New York: Yearling.

Crazy Weekend. (2002). New York: Persea.

The Pool Party. (1993). New York: Yearling.

Summer on Wheels. (1995). New York: Scholastic.

PLAYS

Novio Boy: A Play. (1997). San Diego: Harcourt.

SHORT STORIES

Baseball in April. (1992). New York: Point.
Local News. (1994). New York: Point.
Petty Crimes. (2006). San Diego: Harcourt.

TECHNOLOGY LINKS

For more information about author Gary Soto on the Internet, visit these sites:
  http://www.garysoto.com
  http://www.english.upenn.edu/~afilreis/88/soto-how-things-work.html
This site has links of all kinds, an especially good resource for teachers:
  http://falcon.jmu.edu/~ramseyil/soto.htm

The Maze

by Will Hobbs

Life is a maze at times, with each of us searching the best path to take. Especially as adolescents, when troubles sometimes feel overwhelming, the desire to just fly above and beyond the trouble is strong. Or, as it says on the front cover of this novel, "When your life is a maze, you need wings."

Life literally becomes a maze for Rick Walker. While serving a six-month sentence in a Nevada youth detention center, he believes his life is in jeopardy. Rick escapes, only to find himself in a national park that has a section called the Maze. There, he finds a conservationist whose life as a youth paralleled Rick's. Ironically, it is in the actual Maze that Rick realizes that he has freed himself from the metaphorical one.

This novel provides ample opportunity to talk with students about how one's past certainly influences one's future but does not have to define it; this is a message many students need to hear. The way out of the maze? A willingness to form significant relationships, even friendships, with those who are willing to help.

Will Hobbs is one of today's most celebrated writers for middle-grade students who have a love of adventure. Originally a reading and language arts teacher, he became a full-time writer in 1990.

STANDARDS: IRA/NCTE Standards 1, 3, 4, 5, 6, 11, and 12; NCSS Standards III, IV, V, VI, VII, VIII, and X

MATERIALS

✔ Hobbs, W. (1999). *The Maze.* New York: Camelot. (one per student)

✔ Yolen, J. (1991). *Wings.* San Diego: Harcourt Brace. (one per student)

✔ D'Aulaire, I., & D'Aulaire, E. (1962). *D'Aulaire's Book of Greek Myths.* New York: Doubleday.

✔ Build a Character Think Sheet (page 52, one per student)

FEATURED READING COMPREHENSION STRATEGIES: Text-to-Text Connections, Character Analysis, Visualize

TEXT-TO-TEXT CONNECTIONS

KEY BENEFIT
Comprehension can be enhanced by making a text-to-text connection (Keene & Zimmerman, 1997), one text supporting the understanding of another.

Scholastic Teaching Resources: Teaching Reading Strategies With Literature That Matters to Middle Schoolers 52

Build a Character Think Sheet

As you read this novel, keep track of Rick's actions and thoughts, noting the pages where you find them. Then, write one word or phrase that describes them. For example, in the opening chapter, Rick never gets around to telling the judge he's sorry. This situation may show that Rick is "stubborn" or that he has "excessive pride." Document as much evidence as possible as you read.

ACTIONS	THOUGHTS
Quick description _____	Quote _____
Possible trait _____ Page ___	Possible trait _____ Page ___
Quick description _____	Quote _____
Possible trait _____ Page ___	Possible trait _____ Page ___
Quick description _____	Quote _____
Possible trait _____ Page ___	Possible trait _____ Page ___
Quick description _____	Quote _____
Possible trait _____ Page ___	Possible trait _____ Page ___
Quick description _____	Quote _____
Possible trait _____ Page ___	Possible trait _____ Page ___
Quick description _____	Quote _____
Possible trait _____ Page ___	Possible trait _____ Page ___

L	aw-abiding
O	bservant
N	eat

or

L	iving with the condors
O	pen-hearted toward Rick
N	ever lonely

Before Reading

1. Read aloud Jane Yolen's *Wings*, the mythological story of Daedelus and his son Icarus, and discuss its possible lessons. Ask students to keep this story in mind as they read *The Maze*.

2. As a class, have students create a definition of *loyalty*. Then complete a Venn diagram illustrating how the two concepts, friendship and loyalty, are similar and different.

During Reading

CHARACTER ANALYSIS

1. In Chapter 1, the judge asks, "Who is Rick Walker?" As students read the rest of the novel, ask them to use the Build a Character Think Sheet to keep a list of character traits.

2. In Chapter 15, Lon explains to Rick why he changed his name from Kenny McDermott to Lon Peregrino. Ask students to use Lon's new name to write an acrostic poem that describes how Lon is, indeed, like a peregrine falcon. Create the acrostic by writing Lon's name vertically, one letter per line. Then, using each letter, write a word or phrase describing Lon.
See examples at left:

VISUALIZE

3. Ask students to form small groups and draw a picture of how thermals support gliding. They can use information from the book as well as any other information they find. Then, have each group present their drawings to the class.

After Reading

1. Ask students to think about whether or not Rick "got off easy," whether the revision of his "sentence" was appropriate. After a whole-class discussion, ask students to form pairs or small groups to write a persuasive paragraph or essay explaining their position.

2. When Lon is watching Maverick one day, he exclaims that M-4 is "born to fly." Of course, a condor is literally "born to fly." Ask students what they were born to do. Have students write a goal statement on an index card or print one out on the computer about their aspirations for their futures and create a "Born to . . ." bulletin board. Afterward, discuss with them how they would complete that phrase for Rick.

3. Rick loves to read mythology. Ask students to read a myth of their choice and then retell it to their classmates. They might want to consult *D'Aulaire's Book of Greek Myths*.

Extension Activities

- What other animals or habitats are in danger? Invite students to brainstorm responses to this question. Next, as a class, check out a Web site like that of the Turner Endangered Species Fund (http://tesf.org/). Then, in small groups, students should choose one animal or issue to investigate further and share results with the class.

- At one point in the novel, the guess is that Nuke and Carlile are smuggling out pottery created by the Anasazi people. Have the class find out more about this native group. In small groups students should research a particular topic, such as location, housing, lifestyle, dress, and arts.

- When Rick asks Lon whether the "Buffalo Gals" in the song he's always singing are girls or female buffaloes, Lon says he doesn't know. An interested student or two can find out the history of that song and share it with the class.

- Students can choose another of Hobbs's books to read, and present a book talk.

Further Reading

More books by Will Hobbs:

Beardance. (1999). New York: Camelot.

Bearstone. (1997). New York: Camelot.

The Big Wander. (1994). New York: Camelot.

Changes in Latitude. (1994). New York: Flare.

Crossing the Wire. (2006). New York: HarperCollins.

Down the Yukon. (2001). New York: HarperTrophy.

Downriver. (1996). New York: Dell.

Far North. (1997). New York: Camelot.

Ghost Canoe. (1998). New York: Camelot.

Jason's Gold. (2000). New York: HarperTrophy.

Kokopelli's Flute. (1997). New York: Camelot.

River Thunder. (1999). New York: Laurel-Leaf.

Wild Man Island. (2002). New York: HarperCollins.

TECHNOLOGY LINKS

For more information about author Will Hobbs on the Internet, visit these sites:

http://www.willhobbsauthor.com

http://www.edupaperback.org/showauth2.cfm?authid=253

These sites have more information about the California condor and/or address the conservation projects associated with the condor:

http://arnica.csustan.edu/esrpp/condor.htm

http://www.peregrinefund.org

http://www.pbs.org/wnet/nature/attractions/condors.html

http://www.lazoo.org/condorall

For general information on endangered species visit:

http://endangered.fws.gov

Because of Winn-Dixie

by Kate DiCamillo

How does a lonely girl find friendship in a new town? It's easy when her kind heart and "smiling" dog lead her to some unexpected places and realizations.

Quick thinking helps 10-year-old India Opal Buloni rescue a stray dog from certain punishment for the havoc he wreaks in the produce section of a grocery store. Claiming ownership of the unknown canine, she instantly dubs him "Winn-Dixie" and the two become inseparable companions. Adjusting to her new home in Naomi, Florida, while trying to connect with her preoccupied but loving preacher father, India finds friends among an unlikely assortment of people—and it's all because of Winn-Dixie. This charming, easy-to-read story will capture the hearts of middle schoolers, who will quickly identify with India's quest for family and friends. Each chapter reads like a short story and can be discussed as such, within the context of the larger novel.

STANDARDS: IRA/NCTE Standards: 1, 2, 3, 5, 6, 7, 8, 9, 11, and 12; NCSS Standards I, IV, and X

MATERIALS

✔ DiCamillo, K. (2000). *Because of Winn-Dixie*. Cambridge, MA: Candlewick Press. (one per student)

✔ Sticky-notes

✔ Drawing paper

✔ Opal's Friendship Chart (page 53, one per student)

FEATURED READING COMPREHENSION STRATEGIES: Predict; Visualize; Determine Importance

Before Reading

1. The book's title will pique students' curiosity. Have them hypothesize about its possible implications and record their responses on a prediction chart. Read aloud or have students independently read Chapters 1 and 2, in which Opal finds Winn-Dixie and takes him home.

During Reading

1. After reading the first two chapters, have students confirm or refute their predictions. Then divide the class into groups of four or five. Instruct them to discuss the story so far—characters, setting, favorite scenes, and so on—and decide which elements are the most important. Have each group member select one of the elements to illustrate and describe in writing. For example, students may draw their mental images of India Opal, Winn-Dixie (the store, the dog, or both!), the preacher (India's father), the Open Arms Baptist Church, or the Friendly Corners Trailer Park (India's home). Such exercises encourage visualization—an important component of comprehension. Groups should then sequence their completed illustrations in the appropriate order and share them with the rest of the class. Exhibit each group's work in a "wall story" display (Hoyt, 2002). Discuss key significant points of the chapters that students may have overlooked.

2. As the class continues to read the book, provide students with sticky-notes and instructions to mark words, phrases, or paragraphs they consider important or interesting. Groups should meet occasionally to discuss their notes and to supplement their wall stories with more illustrations and captions.

DETERMINE IMPORTANCE

After Reading

1. Discuss the characters Opal befriends in the story: Miss Franny, the elderly librarian; Otis, the slow-witted pet store manager; Gloria Dump, the town "witch"; Amanda Wilkinson, a sullen classmate; and, of course, Winn-Dixie.

2. Distribute Opal's Friendship Chart on which students should list Opal's friends. Students can use the Think, Pair, Share structure to complete the chart independently, partner with a classmate to discuss their work, and finally, share their thoughts with the entire class. As necessary, help students realize the variety of human characteristics represented in this book.

3. Middle schoolers will likely be very accepting of these characters' quirks and flaws. Guide them, however, in analyzing their attitudes toward individuals in their own school and community who exemplify similar characteristics. In small- or large-groups, discuss

   - *Do you consider such people "friendship material?" Why or why not?*

   - *What common characteristics do people share that make them deserving of our friendship and affection?*

   - *Why is it important to look beyond surface attributes?*

   - *Do we sometimes wrongly prejudge people who may make worthy friends? Why?*

   - *What are the characteristics of a good friend? What needs do they fulfill?*

   Have students develop personal friendship charts similar to Opal's and discuss them. Challenge students to enrich their lives by uncovering the friendship potential in someone they may typically ignore.

Opal's Friendship Chart

	What Others Saw	What Opal Saw	Characteristics That Made Each a Friend
Miss Frannie			
Otis			
Gloria Dump			
Amanda			
Winn-Dixie			

Scholastic Teaching Resources: Teaching Reading Strategies With Literature That Matters to Middle Schoolers, 53

Extension Activities

- India Opal's name reflects both her father's history as a missionary in India and his mother's name. Ask students to investigate the origin of their name, as well as the meaning behind it.

- Direct students to write in a journal entry, as Opal does in the novel, ten things about a person they love. Encourage students to share the list with that person.

- The author has used a number of effective similes and metaphors in this story. An especially telling one is Opal's description of her father: "Sometimes he reminded me of a turtle hiding inside its shell, in there thinking about things and not ever sticking his head out into the world" (p. 16). As a class, locate this and other figures of speech in the novel and discuss their effectiveness in communicating the author's meaning.

Further Reading

Bauer, Joan. (2000). *Hope Was Here.* New York: Putnam.
Creech, Sharon. (1996). *Walk Two Moons.* New York: HarperTrophy.
Horvath, Polly. (2001). *Everything on a Waffle.* New York: Farrar, Straus & Giroux.

TECHNOLOGY LINKS

The American Library Association's Newbery Medal home page:
  http://www.ala.org/alsc/newbery.html

Maniac Magee
by Jerry Spinelli

Maniac Magee is the story of a kid, "one part fact, two parts legend, and three parts snowball," according to author Jerry Spinelli. It's the story of a guy who knew how to be a friend—with anyone. Maniac, born Jeffrey Lionel Magee, lost his parents in a high-speed trolley accident when he was 3 years old. Afterward, he lived with his aunt and uncle in a truly dysfunctional household; his aunt and uncle hated each other but would not divorce for religious reasons. Consequently, they lived parallel lives, eventually having two of virtually everything: two TVs, two toasters, two refrigerators. Even Maniac was "split"; if he ate dinner with Aunt Dot on Monday, he ate dinner with Uncle Dan on Tuesday, and so on. After eight years, Jeffrey had had enough. In the middle of his school's spring musicale, Jeffrey screamed at his aunt and uncle, "Talk! Talk, will ya! Talk! Talk! Talk!" and then he ran out of the auditorium. The legendary life of Maniac had begun.

Maniac Magee won the Newbery award in 1991. Spinelli's ability to draw in the reader by creating characters who seem almost real became his trademark. The reader comes to believe that Maniac, despite his less than auspicious beginnings, and the troubles that surface within the novel, ultimately will be okay, and that one is richer for having had Maniac as a friend. Maniac is an amazing athlete, avid reader, and steadfast friend. He is "colorblind"; he doesn't see difference—just people. The power of friendship across differences makes for a highly memorable reading experience.

STANDARDS: IRA/NCTE Standards 1, 3, 4, 6, 9, 11, and 12; NCSS Standards I, IV, and X

> **MATERIALS**
>
> ✔ Spinelli, J. (1990). *Maniac Magee*. Boston: Little, Brown. (one per student)
>
> ✔ Reading Like a Writer (page 54, one per student)

FEATURED READING COMPREHENSION STRATEGIES: Preview; Examine Text Structure; Text-to-Self Connections

Before Reading

1. Read aloud the three-page preface called "Before the Story." Ask students why they think Spinelli wrote this short section.

2. Ask students to preview the structure of this novel. As they page through, they will probably notice that although this book has conventional, consecutively numbered chapters, it also has three divisions: Parts I, II, and III. Ask students to predict why the novel may be designed this way. Record their predictions so that they can reconsider this question after finishing the novel.

PREVIEW

During Reading

1. Spinelli is a master of pulling the reader from one chapter to the next: He uses a solid hook that foreshadows what's coming. The common cry at the end of reading aloud each chapter is "Go on. Read the next chapter." For example, read the last two lines of Chapter 16, "And Maniac couldn't see it [the dislike]. And then all of a sudden he could" (p. 58). "How?" the reader demands. Ask students to find other examples of this technique, in this novel or in others.

EXAMINE TEXT STRUCTURE

2. Similar to the chapter-to-chapter hooks, the author also creates internal reading guides. For example, in Chapter 4, Spinelli writes, "Jeffrey made three other appearances that first day." He describes the first one in the rest of Chapter 4, the second in Chapter 5, and the third in Chapter 6. He provides ongoing support for the reader with such intermittent scaffolds. Again, ask students to find examples of this technique. Discuss with them how this technique helps the reader. Ask them to explain why they should think about doing this in their own writing.

3. As students are reading through the text, provide them with sticky-notes. When they find a passage that really speaks to them in some way have them place their sticky-note right on those words so they can share it during a class discussion about Spinelli's language. For example, a student may read aloud the text on page 54 beginning with "The new white kid" and ending with "Hallelujah! A-men!" because he liked the way Spinelli's repetition of "who" accentuates how Maniac's fame spread all over the East End.

   Another student may choose this passage, explaining that Spinelli's sentence fragments, make reading it really sound like teeth chattering: "A faint, tiny noise. A rattling. A chittering. A chattering. And getting louder—yes—chattering teeth. Arnold Jones's teeth. They're chattering like snare drums" (p. 18).

   Or a student may just chose a word like *finsterwallies,* saying she or he likes it because Spinelli made it up, and the word seems to fit his definition perfectly: "violent trembling of the body, especially in the extremities (arms and legs)" (p. 18).

Reading Like a Writer

Jerry Spinelli uses dashes to slow the pace of the words, which emphasizes his point. What point is he emphasizing in these examples?

1. "No, he was running—running—where the Pickwells themselves, where every other kid, had only ever walked—on the steel rail itself!" (p. 21).

_____

2. "Just that—'Hi'—and he was gone" (p. 9).

_____

3. Find your own example of a place when Spinelli uses dashes and then describe why you believe he does so.

Example: _____

_____

Reason: _____

_____

The author uses an ellipsis, a set of three periods, to emphasize the passage of time. What point is he emphasizing in these examples?

1. As McNab is striking out batters, Spinelli writes: "Twenty-six! . . . Twenty-seven! . . . Twenty-eight! . . . He was like a shark. Thirty-four! . . . Thirty-five! . . ." (p. 35).

_____

_____

2. "The nightmare was worse than ever. I saw the trolley coming . . . I saw it . . . f-falling . . . them . . . them . . ." (p. 176).

3. Find your own example of a place when Spinelli uses an ellipsis or a series of ellipses and then describe why you believe he does so.

Example: _____

_____

Reason: _____

_____

Spinelli uses colons frequently, too. What effect does this kind of punctuation have on his prose? Why would he use a colon instead of a semi-colon?

1. "He [McNab] roared: 'Get my hat! Get the ball!'" (p. 24).

2. "Mrs. Pickwell did better: she treated him like a member of the family, as if she would have been surprised if he hadn't come on the whistle" (p. 153).

3. Find your own example of a place when Spinelli uses a colon and then describe why you believe he does so.

Example: _____

_____

Reason: _____

Scholastic Teaching Resources: Teaching Reading Strategies With Literature That Matters to Middle Schoolers 54

KEY BENEFIT

Middle-grade writers are eager to use more "exotic" forms of punctuation such as dashes, ellipses, and colons. While traditional wisdom maintains that more conventional forms should be mastered first, promoting the palette of options "real" writers use may help middle-grade students be more aware of all the tools writers use.

After Reading

1. By dividing the book into three parts, the author makes apparent Maniac's three "lives" in the story. Divide the class into small groups (three, if possible). Ask each group to write a summary of the main events in one of the parts. Once groups have shared, ask them to give their part of the book a name. Students should come to realize that Spinelli's division of the book parallels Maniac's life, first with the Beales, then with Grayson, and finally with the McNabs.

2. As middle-grade readers begin to appreciate the conventions of language, they won't mind a bit if Maniac helps show the way. Using Reading Like a Writer, help students notice more about Spinelli's playfulness with language.

3. In the middle section of the book, Maniac's friend Grayson discovers that Maniac uses his lunch money to buy books that the library is discarding. When Maniac shows Grayson his collection of "ancient, back-broken math books, flaking travel books, warped spellers, mangled mysteries, biographies, music books, astronomy books, cookbooks," Grayson asks, "Can't you make up your mind what kind you want?" Maniac responds, "I want them all. I'm learning everything!" (p. 98). Ask students to characterize their "libraries." Ask them to make a list of their special books. Have them look for patterns in their lists, and then write a paragraph describing their collections.

TEXT-TO-SELF CONNECTIONS

4. *Maniac Magee* is at its heart a story about prejudice. Reminiscent of Mark Twain's *Adventures of Huckleberry Finn*, when Huck realizes that Jim has human feelings, too, Spinelli addresses the issue in a dialog between Grayson and Maniac on pages 87–89. Again, it is a young person who holds the enlightened perspective. Have students comment on this perspective, finding other examples in the text when Maniac either misses or notices prejudice. Ask students what they think Spinelli's purpose is in exploring this theme.

Extension Activities

- When Maniac asks for a bedtime story, Grayson says he doesn't know any. Maniac tells him of course he does, "Everybody has a story" (p. 89). Invite students to write their story. Ask for volunteers to share.

- At one point, Maniac is living on the streets, visiting places like the Salvation Army for food. Homelessness is one of America's tragedies. As a class, investigate the issue of homelessness in your local community. Ask students to consider these tough questions:

  - *Who are the homeless?*

  - *How did they come to be homeless?*

  - *What options do these people have, especially if cold weather is an issue, as it was for Maniac?*

  - *What could you do to ease the lives of people in this situation?*

- Have students choose another of Spinelli's book to read, and then present a book talk to the class.

Further Reading

More books by Jerry Spinelli:

NOVELS

Crash. (1996). New York: Knopf.
Dump Days. (1988). Boston: Little, Brown.
Jason and Marceline. (1986). Boston: Little, Brown.
The Library Card. (1997). New York: Scholastic.
Loser. (2002). New York: Joanna Cotler Books.
Milkweed. (2003). New York: Knopf Books for Young Readers.
School Daze: Do the Funky Pickle. (1992). New York: Scholastic.
School Daze: Picklemania. (1993). New York: Scholastic.
School Daze: Report to the Principal's Office. (1991). New York: Scholastic.
School Daze: Who Ran My Underwear up the Flagpole? (1992). New York: Scholastic.
Space Station Seventh Grade. (1982). Boston: Little, Brown.
Who Put That Hair in My Toothbrush? (1984). Boston: Little, Brown.
Wringer. (1997). New York: HarperCollins.

AUTOBIOGRAPHY

Knots in My Yo-Yo String: The Autobiography of a Kid. (1998). New York: Knopf.

TECHNOLOGY LINKS

For more information about author Jerry Spinelli, visit this site:
   http://www.edupaperback.org/showauth2.cfm?authid=74

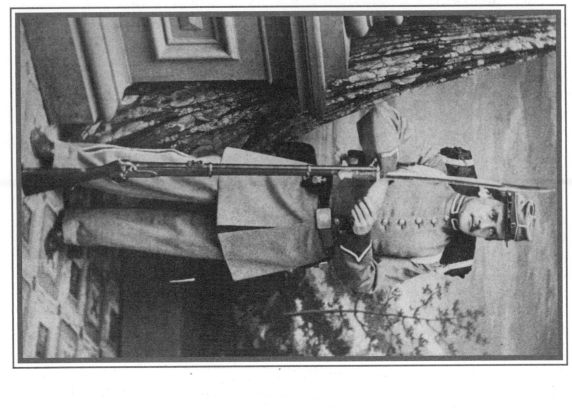

Confederate Soldier

Union Soldier

Quick Summary Think Sheet

After you read each chapter, write a title for it, summarizing the key idea.

Chapter 1 _____

Chapter 2 _____

Chapter 3 _____

Chapter 4 _____

Chapter 5 _____

Chapter 6 _____

Chapter 7 _____

Chapter 8 _____

Chapter 9 _____

Chapter 10 _____

Chapter 11 _____

Chapter 12 _____

Chapter 13 _____

Build a Character Think Sheet

As you read this novel, keep track of Rick's actions and thoughts, noting the pages where you find them. Then, write one word or phrase that describes them. For example, in the opening chapter, Rick never gets around to telling the judge he's sorry. This situation may show that Rick is "stubborn" or that he has "excessive pride." Document as much evidence as possible as you read.

ACTIONS

Quick description _____

Possible trait _____ Page ___

Quick description _____

Possible trait _____ Page ___

Quick description _____

Possible trait _____ Page ___

Quick description _____

Possible trait _____ Page ___

Quick description _____

Possible trait _____ Page ___

Quick description _____

Possible trait _____ Page ___

Quick description _____

Possible trait _____ Page ___

THOUGHTS

Quote _____

Possible trait _____ Page ___

Quote _____

Possible trait _____ Page ___

Quote _____

Possible trait _____ Page ___

Quote _____

Possible trait _____ Page ___

Quote _____

Possible trait _____ Page ___

Quote _____

Possible trait _____ Page ___

Quote _____

Possible trait _____ Page ___

Opal's Friendship Chart

	What Others Saw	What Opal Saw	Characteristics That Made Each a Friend
Miss Frannie			
Otis			
Gloria Dump			
Amanda			
Winn-Dixie			

Reading Like a Writer

Jerry Spinelli uses dashes to slow the pace of the words, which emphasizes his point. What point is he emphasizing in these examples?

1. "No, he was running—running—where the Pickwells themselves, where every other kid, had only ever walked—on the steel rail itself!" (p. 21).

_____

_____

2. "Just that—'Hi'—and he was gone" (p. 9).

_____

_____

3. Find your own example of a place when Spinelli uses dashes and then describe why you believe he does so.

Example: _____

_____

_____

Reason: _____

_____

_____

The author uses an ellipsis, a set of three periods, to emphasize the passage of time. What point is he emphasizing in these examples?

1. As McNab is striking out batters, Spinelli writes: "Twenty-six! . . . Twenty-seven! . . . Twenty-eight! . . . He was like a shark. Thirty-four! . . . Thirty-five! . . ." (p. 35).

_____

_____

_____

2. "The nightmare was worse than ever. I saw the trolley coming . . . I saw it . . . f-falling . . . them . . . them . . ." (p. 176).

_____

_____

3. Find your own example of a place when Spinelli uses an ellipsis or a series of ellipses and then describe why you believe he does so.

Example: _____

_____

Reason: _____

_____

Spinelli uses colons frequently, too. What effect does this kind of punctuation have on his prose? Why would he use a colon instead of a semi-colon?

1. "He [McNab] roared: "Get my hat! Get the ball!" (p. 24).

_____

_____

2. "Mrs. Pickwell did better: she treated him like a member of the family, as if she would have been surprised if he hadn't come on the whistle" (p. 153).

_____

_____

3. Find your own example of a place when Spinelli uses a colon and then describe why you believe he does so.

Example: _____

_____

Reason: _____

_____

Chapter 3

Making Choices

Fundamental to forging one's identity are the choices a person makes along the way. Parents and teachers hope the children in their charge will navigate adolescence using good judgment. They hope that positive role models and frank dialogue provide middle schoolers with a much-needed moral compass for guiding responsible decision making. The literature in this chapter supplies many of those role models and complex situations that require reasoned choices: Should I do this? Should I not? What are the consequences? Is it ever right to do the "wrong" thing? What are the potential costs to me? To others? Are people ever forced by their lack of options to make seemingly impossible decisions? Do the ends justify the means? Many of the learning activities that follow provide opportunities for students to discuss the black, white, and gray areas of ethical decision making and, most important, learn that difficult choices should be grounded in personal conviction and reflection.

The Butterfly

by Patricia Polacco

Although a picture book, this offering from Patricia Polacco deals with a serious subject: the plight of Jews during the Nazi occupation of Paris during World War II. Once again, the author draws on her own family history, telling the story of her great-aunt Marcel, who bravely chose to shelter Jewish families in her home. Polacco treats a difficult topic gently but honestly, and though the book is targeted toward younger students, its content and vocabulary (including French and German words) make it entirely fitting for older students.

Young Monique wakes from her sleep one night to discover a "ghost child" sitting on the edge of her bed. She soon discovers that the girl is not a ghost at all, but the child of a Jewish family hiding in her basement. Though incredulous at first that an entire family could be living there without her knowledge, she quickly befriends the child, Sevrine, and the two begin to meet secretly at night after their families have gone to sleep.

Knowing that Sevrine cannot venture into the outside world, Monique brings her gifts—a handful of earth, a flower, and a butterfly—small tokens of nature that symbolizes the freedom she wishes for her new friend. When the girls inadvertently allow themselves to be discovered by a neighbor one night, Monique quickly grasps the gravity of their situation and rouses her mother to tell her all. Marcel hurriedly arranges for the family to leave Paris, and the remainder of the story describes their escape and subsequent fates.

STANDARDS: IRA/NCTE Standards: 1, 2, 3, 7, 8, 9, 10, 11, and 12; NCSS Standards I, II, III, IV, and VI

MATERIALS

✔ Polacco, P. (2000). *The Butterfly.* New York: Scholastic. (one per student)

✔ Photos of the Eiffel Tower and swastika emblem (page 70)

✔ World map

✔ Computer with Internet access

FEATURED READING COMPREHENSION STRATEGIES: Background Knowledge; Infer; Graphic Organizer: T-Chart

Before Reading

Note: Remove the photo of the German building if you do not plan to have a discussion about its historical context.

BACKGROUND KNOWLEDGE

1. Distribute copies of the Eiffel Tower photo. Ask students to identify it: *Can anyone tell me what this is and where you might see it?* Discuss the fact that Paris is famous for this landmark as well as many others. To build background knowledge, allow

students to comment on other aspects of French culture with which they are familiar. Tell students that the lovely city of Paris has had difficult times in its history and that one of those occurred during World War II when it was occupied by German troops.

Scholastic Teaching Resources: Teaching Reading Strategies With Literature That Matters to Middle Schoolers 70

2. Bring students' attention to the photo of the building with the symbol (swastika). Again, ask students if they recognize it and its meaning. Facilitate a discussion about this symbol that is appropriate for your students' ages. Include terms like *Nazi, Jews,* and *the Holocaust.* Use a map to point out Germany and show its proximity to France. Tell students that they are going to be viewing a video and reading a story about two different children, one who lived in Paris during the war and the other who lived in Germany.

KEY BENEFIT

"A picture is worth a thousand words" the adage states, and it's probably true. The motivation and support for reading that photographs or illustrations provide should never be underestimated.

3. Ask students, *Have you ever been punished for something you didn't do?* Briefly discuss, and then pay a virtual visit to the U.S. Holocaust Museum in Washington, D.C. Among its many powerful teaching tools is a ten-minute video, "Remember the Children: Daniel's Story," in which a Jewish man tells the story of his youth, when his family was sent to a Jewish ghetto, then to a concentration camp. He repeats the question, "Have you ever been punished for something you didn't do?" The video is supported by written text and makes clear the meaning of the word *Nazi.*

4. Display the back cover of *The Butterfly*, on which Polacco has drawn a full-page illustration of a Nazi soldier with the swastika prominently displayed both on his uniform and on the flag behind him. Discuss the soldier and what his presence might signify to the citizens of Paris. Then, direct students' attention to the front cover and ask students to describe what they see: a sad-faced girl staring at the soldier and flag, but with a butterfly and flowers in the background behind her. Encourage students to speculate about what these contradictory illustrations may mean. If desired, lead students on a picture walk through the book's illustrations, noting the appearances of the swastika and butterfly throughout. Emphasize that what they are about to hear is a true story.

INFER

During or After Reading

1. Create a T-chart on the board or overhead, labeling one side "Situation" and the other side "Characters' Choices." Discuss pivotal points in the story and encourage students to consider the choices—or lack of choices—that the characters have in each situation. See the example on the next page.

57

SITUATION	CHARACTERS' CHOICES
Monique discovers Sevrine ("the ghost child") in her room.	Sevrine has chosen to leave basement and sneak into Monique's room; Monique chooses to tell her mother about her "dream." Marcel chooses not to tell Monique that she is hiding a Jewish family in their basement.
Monique discovers Sevrine in her room.	Sevrine chooses to stay and visit with Monique. Monique again chooses not to tell her mother.
The two girls meet nightly in Monique's room.	Monique chooses to protect her friend by keeping their visits a secret.
Monique brings Sevrine a butterfly.	Sevrine chooses to free it.

Analyze with students the implications of each decision or choice:

- *Did the characters choose well? What were the ultimate results?*

- *Why do you think some people choose wisely and unselfishly while others make foolish or selfish choices?*

- *What are the consequences of poor choices? How do they affect individuals and the people around them?*

- *By what criteria should we make our choices?*

Extension Activities

- Students can use the extensive learning tools available on the U.S. Holocaust Museum's Web site to learn about other survivors' stories, view the Hall of Remembrance, and more.

- Have students explore "The Holocaust: A Tragic Legacy," an interactive ThinkQuest. They can access the site's home page to read a summary of the Holocaust, hear survivors' stories, view a time line, and participate in scenarios in which they are confronted with life-or-death situations during the Holocaust and have to choose what to do. Ask volunteers to share their responses.

- Watch the documentary *Into the Arms of Strangers: Stories of the Kindertransport* (2000), narrated by Dame Judi Dench. Discuss links between these stories and that of *The Butterfly.* Students can create a classroom Wall of Remembrance with "tiles" they design and dedicate to a child who was a victim of the Holocaust.

Further Reading

NOVELS
Frank, A. (1993). *Anne Frank: The Diary of a Young Girl*. New York: Bantam.
Lowry, L. (1988). *Number the Stars*. New York: Houghton Mifflin.
Yolen, J. (1987). *The Devil's Arithmetic*. New York: Viking.

PICTURE BOOKS
Innocenti, R. (1996). *Rose Blanche*. San Diego: Harcourt.

TECHNOLOGY LINKS
Visit ThinkQuest's "The Holocaust: A Tragic Legacy":
   http://library.thinkquest.org/12663/
The U.S. Holocaust Museum's Web site:
   http://www.ushmm.org

Note to teacher: Because this book is set in the South in 1956, the n-word is used several times. Students should be prepared for its use.

Speed of Light
by Sybil Rosen

> "Dr. Einstein was right. You could live a whole lifetime in a second sometimes when you traveled at the speed of light" (p. 169).

Thus ends the story of 11-year-old Audrey Ina's summer in Blue Gap, Virginia, in 1956. This summer is a pivotal one for Audrey—she learns much about the world and how she relates to people in it. The key event is her father's support for one of his employees' efforts to become the town's first black police officer. The townspeople are not happy that a Jewish man is actively challenging segregation. Why would a Jewish man want to change the order of things? Even his brother questions his wisdom, scared of the repercussions of his actions. But Audrey's father responds, "How else do I teach them right from wrong unless I do what I believe is right myself?" This historical novel supports the chapter "Making Choices" because the father is making active choices, actually doing what he believes is right. Not only is he an excellent role model for his children, he sets an excellent example for all of us.

STANDARDS: IRA/NCTE Standards 1, 2, 3, 4, 7, 8, 9, 11, and 12; NCSS Standards I, II, IV, V, VI, and X

MATERIALS

✔ Rosen, S. (1999). *Speed of Light*. New York: Simon & Schuster. (one per student)

✔ Index cards

✔ Cool Words think sheets (pages 71 and 72, one each per student)

FEATURED READING COMPREHENSION STRATEGIES: Background Knowledge; Context Clues; Journal

Before Reading

1. Ask students to respond to this question on an index card by voting "everything," "nothing," or "something": *What does another person's suffering have to do with me?* Have students put their names on the other side of the cards. Use the cards to make a graph on the board. Compute the percentages. Ask volunteers to share their perspectives, and if appropriate, ask them to elaborate by responding to this question: *And what can I do about it?*

2. Preview the online magazine *The Ethical Spectacle*. If you believe it to be suitable for your class, share the introduction to the "Auschwitz Alphabet," written by the magazine's editor, Jonathan Blument (http://www.spectacle.org/695/ausch.html). Then, assign each student a letter, or allow them to choose one, and ask them to visit that letter of his alphabet. This will provide background knowledge for stu-

**BACKGROUND
KNOWLEDGE**

KEY BENEFIT

The "Cool Words" strategy encourages students to use their background knowledge and context clues to determine the meaning of unfamiliar words, following Pearson's (1984) advice to try not to "put" new words into students' heads but help students determine what they already know as a way of refining their understandings.

dents so that they understand Tante Pesel's past and her difficulties with the turmoil in the novel. Ask them to summarize what they have learned and share it with their classmates.

3. For further information, ask students to visit the official Web site for the Auschwitz Birkenow Memorial and Museum, which also has plentiful links: http://www.auschwitz-muzeum.oswiecim.pl.

During Reading

1. If you would like students to explore Einstein's theory of relativity more fully after reading about him in Chapter 5, show them the "Think Like Einstein" link on the PBS Web site, at http://www.pbs.org/wgbh/nova/time/think.html. Help them think of questions that could be included and then answer the questions together. Then, as a class, check to see if they already are on the Web site.

2. Audrey uses sophisticated language at times. Using the Cool Words Think Sheet, explore the four words listed there and then challenge students to find others from the book. Make sure students have a chance to share their favorite cool word with the class.

CONTEXT CLUES

After Reading

1. Ask students to consider once more the questions: *What does another person's suffering have to do with me?* and *What can I do about it?* and respond in a journal entry. Encourage them to explain whether their answer has changed, or changed in intensity. Ask them how considering these questions encourages them to make good choices.

JOURNAL

2. Albert Einstein was chosen as *Time* magazine's Person of the Century. Ask students to visit *Time*'s Web page dedicated to him, http://www.time.com/time/time100/poc/home.html, and then make a case either supporting *Time*'s choice or making a case for someone else. Students may be particularly interested in the "Q and A About Relativity" in the Gravity Probe B section of "Network Resources."

3. In Chapter 14, Audrey and her dad have an important conversation about compassion after Buster throws rocks at her and Sam. Discuss their conversation in terms of "making choices." Stress how each person ultimately makes his or her own choices and creates his or her own happiness or unhappiness.

Extension Activities

- Visit the online art collection "Last Expression: Art from Auschwitz" at: http://lastexpression.northwestern.edu/exhibition_fr_search.html. Click on "Search Art," and look at the pictures carefully. Choose one and then respond to it in a poetic way. Create a display in the school to showcase your writing.

- The stars fascinate Audrey. Research the constellations and stars that Audrey knows, such as Bootes, Arcturus, Cygnus, Polaris, the North Star, the Big Dipper, Sirius, and Perseid. Draw them or create their patterns by pushing a safety pin through a piece of paper. Then show the patterns on an overhead projector. Label both significant stars and the constellations.

- *Speed of Light* won the Sydney Taylor Book Award. Choose another book that's won this award, read it, and then present a book talk to the class.

Further Reading (all Sydney Taylor Book Award winners)

NONFICTION
Adler, D. (1986). *The Numbers on My Grandfather's Arm*. New York: UAHC Press.
Meltzer, M. (1975). *Never to Forget*. New York: Harper & Row.
Reef, C. (2000). *Sigmund Freud: Pioneer of the Mind*. New York: Clarion.

PICTURE BOOKS
Joestlandt, J. (1994). *Star of Fear, Star of Hope*. New York: Walker and Company.
Polacco, P. (1987). *The Keeping Quilt*. New York: Simon & Schuster.

TRADITIONAL STORIES
Schwartz, H., & Rush, B. (1990). *The Diamond Tree: Jewish Tales From Around the World*. New York: HarperCollins.

NOVELS
Hesse, K. (1991). *Letters From Rifka*. New York: Henry Holt.
Napoli, D. J. (1997). *Stones in Water*. New York: Dutton.
Vos, I. (2000). *The Key Is Lost*. (Therese Edelstein, Trans.). New York: HarperCollins.

TECHNOLOGY LINKS
For more information about the Holocaust, visit:
    http://www.remember.org
For an extensive list of Web sites about Albert Einstein, visit these sites:
    http://www.westegg.com/einstein
    http://www.albert-einstein.org

Shiloh

by Phyllis Reynolds Naylor

A boy and his dog—a classic pairing that has been the subject of television, movies, and even works of art. Naylor's Newbery award–winning novel adds a provocative twist by raising questions about the ethical behavior of humans toward animals and one another.

Marty Preston, the novel's protagonist, unwittingly incurs a problem when a stray beagle follows him home from one of his regular excursions into the nearby West Virginia hills. When, at his father's insistence, Marty reluctantly returns the dog he has named Shiloh to its rightful owner, Judd Travers, his suspicions that the animal has been mistreated are confirmed. Sick with concern about Shiloh, Marty is relieved when the dog once again appears in his yard. The repercussions of his decision to hide Shiloh form the plot of this absorbing book.

It's a rare middle schooler who won't be drawn into the mounting tension as Marty tries to shelter Shiloh and guard his secret from both his family and Judd Travers. To her credit, Naylor is wise enough to avoid oversimplifying her well-drawn characters. Both the protagonist and the antagonist can be defended or accused, which lends authenticity and depth to the story.

STANDARDS: IRA/NCTE STANDARDS 1, 2, 3, 4, 6, 7, 8, 9, 11, and 12; NCSS Standards I, IIII, IV, and X

MATERIALS

✔ Naylor, P. R. (2000). *Shiloh*. Aladdin. (one per student)

✔ Shiloh Think Sheet (Inference Chart) (page 73, one per student)

✔ Drawing paper and crayons/markers

✔ Map of West Virginia

✔ Discussion Web (page 74, one per student)

FEATURED READING COMPREHENSION STRATEGIES: Morphemic Analysis, Infer, Visualize, Evaluate, Graphic Organizer: Discussion Web

MORPHEMIC ANALYSIS

KEY BENEFIT
Discussing derivational patterns or word parts expands students' ability to decode words and discover their meanings, especially when a targeted word begins the conversation.

Before Reading

1. Write the word *dilemma* on the board. Ask students if they know its meaning: a situation in which one must choose between two equally attractive or unattractive alternatives. Point out the morphemic (for meaning) components of the word: *di* is Greek for "two" or "double," and *lemma* means "assumptions." Offer an example of circumstances in which you have had difficulty deciding between two nearly equivalent options. Give students an opportunity to share some examples of their own, and the ways they resolved matters. Tell them to identify Marty's dilemma and evaluate his options as they read the book.

During Reading

1. Read aloud the first page of Chapter One. Ask students what they have learned so far. (Names of family members; Shiloh came that day; Marty is telling the story; the father hunts; and so on.) Tell students that there are some clues about the family the author has suggested, but not clearly stated. Think aloud, modeling how you infer meaning from text: *I can infer that Ma is a typical mother who is annoyed when her children don't eat their dinner properly.* Justify your thinking with support from the text: *She says, "Just once in my life I'd like to see a bite of food go direct from the dish into somebody's mouth without a detour of any kind."* Ask students to identify some inferences they can make from the first page, and require that they, too, make their thinking transparent. Here are some possible responses, along with clues from the text:

INFER

Shiloh Think Sheet

Inference	Text Support	Page/Paragraph
The family lives in a rural area.		
They are not wealthy.		
Marty is compassionate toward animals.		
His father doesn't share his concern.		
Ma is a "typical" mother.		
Other		

Scholastic Teaching Resources: Teaching Reading Strategies With Literature That Matters to Middle Schoolers: 73

- The family lives in a rural area. (Dialect; the father hunts.)

- They are not wealthy. (They are having beans and fried rabbit for their "big Sunday dinner.")

- Marty is compassionate toward animals. (He can't eat the rabbit unless he knows it died immediately when shot.)

- Marty's father doesn't seem to share his concern. (He is matter-of-fact about the rabbit's death and not outwardly sensitive to Marty's apparent discomfort.)

   If students need more support in using this comprehension strategy, distribute the Shiloh Think Sheet, which lists possible inferences, and have them locate the text sections that justify them. Encourage students to add their own. They can discuss their answers in pairs or small groups.

2. Read the second page of Chapter One and ask students if their inferences are correct. *What information is offered?* (The family lives in Friendly, West Virginia, in a four-room house; Marty is eleven; he has a gun, but never shoots at living things.)

3. Tell students to visualize the setting and draw a picture of it. Instruct them to consider the landscape, season, and surroundings. Have them share their finished illustrations with a partner and explain why they have included particular details.

VISUALIZE

4. Provide a map of West Virginia. Have students locate Friendly, Sistersville, and the Ohio River. Discuss the terrain.

5. Before continuing to read, ask students to infer why the author might have wanted the reader to know these things about Marty and his family. *What implications might they have for the story?*

6. When Marty discovers Shiloh in his yard once more, stop reading and instruct students to get in small groups and discuss his situation. Remind them of the word *dilemma*, and tell them to suggest options Marty might consider. Have them evaluate those options and predict their outcomes. This activity, too, can be structured with a chart listing Marty's alternatives and their likely consequences.

EVALUATE

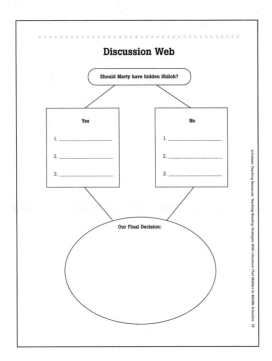

Discussion Web

Should Marty have hidden Shiloh?

Yes

1. _____
2. _____
3. _____

No

1. _____
2. _____
3. _____

Our Final Decision:

Scholastic Teaching Resources: Teaching Reading Strategies With Literature That Matters to Middle Schoolers 74

After Reading

1. Though his intentions are honorable, Marty does something wrong by hiding Shiloh, stealing, and lying. Provide students with the Discussion Web (Alvermann, 1991), which compels them to see the situation from multiple perspectives. Have them work in pairs to critically consider the question posed. Give them five minutes to record three reasons why Marty made the right decision and three reasons why he did not. When time is up, each pair should combine with another pair for ten minutes and discuss their answers. Each group of four should arrive at a consensus and present it and their reasoning to the class.

2. Have students consider how Marty's choice affected his relationships with others, including his family and Judd Travers, Shiloh's owner.

Extension Activities

- Have students investigate dog-licensing requirements in their area. What laws protect animals? How are cases of animal cruelty reported and handled?

- Students can research the economics involved in owning a dog: What costs are involved in feeding and providing health care for pets?

- Secure class copies of the article "The Writing of Shiloh," which appeared in the September 1992 (Vol. 46, No. 1) issue of *The Reading Teacher*. In this adaptation of her Newbery acceptance speech, Phyllis Reynolds Naylor relates the true story that inspired her to create the book. Moreover, she offers insight into her writing process—all of which should be of interest to students.

Further Reading

Students may be interested in reading Naylor's two sequels to *Shiloh*:
Saving Shiloh. (1999). New York: Aladdin.
Shiloh Season. (1999). New York: Aladdin.

OTHER BOOKS

Bunting, E. (2001). *The Summer of Riley*. New York: HarperTrophy.
Creech, S. (2003). *Love That Dog*. New York: HarperTrophy.

TECHNOLOGY LINKS

The American Society for the Prevention of Cruelty to Animals offers information on pet care and ownership costs, as well as real-life animal stories on its Web site: http://www.aspca.org
Phyllis Reynolds Naylor answers frequently asked questions at the Internet Public Library's Kidspace Web site:
http://ipl.si.umich.edu/div/kidspace/askauthor/Naylor.html

The Graduation of Jake Moon

by Barbara Park

Alzheimer's disease. Skelly, Jake's grandfather, has it and it is slowly taking over Skelly's life. Since Jake and his grandfather live together, that also means the disease is also affecting, more and more, Jake's life. Jake is trying to be a good grandson, but the things Skelly does are embarrassing.

The story of the heartbreak of Alzheimer's disease is powerfully told through the eyes of middle grader Jake. Since Skelly is Jake's surrogate father, Jake remembers and honors what Skelly has taught him through the years. Skelly has been a kind, talented, fully competent man who now sometimes puts wet sheets in the oven and pajamas in the freezer. How are Jake and his mom to handle these continual surprises and changes in their beloved father and grandfather?

Jake now has choices to make. Will Jake be there for his grandfather as he has always been for him? Will he honor his grandfather even if he does embarrassing things? Or will Jake ignore him, taking care only of himself? For this heavily peer-influenced age group, this book speaks directly to the impact choices have on determining the essence of our being.

STANDARDS: IRA/NCTE Standards 1, 3, 4, 5, 6, 8, 9, 11, and 12; NCSS Standards IV, V, and VIII

MATERIALS

✔ Park, B. (2000). *The Graduation of Jake Moon*. New York: Atheneum. (one per student)

✔ Dear _____ Think Sheet reproducible (page 75, one per student)

FEATURED READING COMPREHENSION STRATEGIES: Journal; Text-to-Text Connections; Graphic Organizer: Writing Frame

Before Reading

1. Lead a discussion with students about their relationships with grandparents. Ask them:

   • *Do you have a relationship with your grandparents?*

   • *If so, what kinds of activities do you share?*

   • *When do you have a chance to share these activities?*

   • *Do you enjoy the time you spend with your grandparents?*

   • *Do you wish you could spend more time with them?*

2. Read aloud the first chapter, "The Twist." Then, discuss "the twist," or surprise, it reveals. Next, introduce and discuss the literary term *irony*. In literary works, events may be ironic in that they upset the reader's expectations. In this instance, readers may laugh along with Jake and his friends about the man in the garbage can, but they probably stop when they discover that the man is Jake's grandfather.

Students may acknowledge that some things seem funny when we don't know the people involved. It's important to discuss whether such things are truly funny or sad and requiring compassion. Students, hopefully, are surprised that Jake is making fun of his own grandfather. Through discussion, students can come to understand that Jake is wrong to laugh along with his friends and to implicitly deny—by not saying anything—that the man is his grandfather. Hopefully, too, they understand why Jake would do such a thing. Students may be willing to share times when they were less caring than they should have been.

During Reading

JOURNAL

1. In Chapter 2, Jake reports that "Skelly just had that kind of effect on people. He had a way of believing in you, that made you want to believe in yourself" (p. 8). Ask students if they can think of anyone who believes in them that way. Ask them to write a letter thanking that person for being so important in their lives. If not, they can write a letter to someone asking that person to believe in them, and telling this person why this would be an important thing to do.

2. Have students keep a journal as they read as if they were Jake. They should write at least five entries, explaining what Skelly does and their reaction to it.

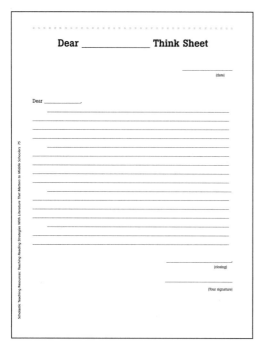

After Reading

TEXT-TO-TEXT CONNECTIONS

1. Jake really didn't like John Steinbeck's *The Pearl*. Invite students to read what is considered a "classic." Then, have them write a book review, comparing their perspective with Jake's.

2. Ask students to explain why the title of the book is *The Graduation of Jake Moon*. Divide the class into small groups to brainstorm other titles. Then have the whole class vote on the one they like best.

Extension Activities

- After students have had a chance to learn more about Alzheimer's disease, have them use the Dear _____ Think Sheet to write a letter to Jake about what they think is the greatest challenge in caring for someone with Alzheimer's and why. They should tie in their response with the theme of this unit, "Making Choices."

- Invite students to choose another of Park's books to read, and then present a book talk to the class.

Further Reading

More books by Barbara Park:

Almost Starring Skinnybones. (1995). New York: Random House.

Beanpole. (1990). New York: Random House.

Don't Make Me Smile. (2002). New York: Random House.

KEY BENEFIT
A writing frame supports reluctant writers by providing a format and definition of acceptable length so that the writing task seems specific and achievable.

The Kid in the Red Jacket. (1995). New York: Random House.
Max, Rosie, and Earl: Partners in Grime. (1991). New York: Random House.
Mick Harte Was Here. (1996). New York: Random House.
Rosie Swanson: Fourth-Grade Geek for President. (1992). New York: Random House.
Skinnybones. (1997). New York: Random House.

TECHNOLOGY LINKS

For more information about author Barbara Park, visit this website:
  http://www.edupaperback.org/showauth2.cfm?authid = 38
For more information about Alzheimer's disease, visit these sites:
  http://www.alzheimers.org
  http://www.alz.co.uk
  http://www.mayoclinic.com

Surviving the Applewhites
by Stephanie Tolan

What does it mean to "survive"? Most middle schoolers are familiar with the survival shows that have become popular additions to television schedules. On these shows, whether in Australia, the Amazon, or Africa, people work hard to have enough to eat and to outwit the other players in order to be the one who lasts the longest and wins the prize. In this novel, Jake does not have to worry about having enough to eat or battling the natural world; he has to survive this alternative school to which he has been sent. When does his perspective change from "surviving" to "thriving"?

Jake is not a typical middle schooler. When he arrives at the Applewhites' Creative Academy, he has "scarlet spiked hair, a silver ring through one dark brown eyebrow, and too many earrings to count. He is dressed entirely in black—black T-shirt, black jeans, black high-top running shoes—and the look in his eyes is pure mean" (p. 1). The Creative Academy is a home school in North Carolina, Jake's "last hope" before he is sent back to juvenile hall in New Jersey.

STANDARDS: IRA/NCTE Standards 1, 3, 4, 5, 7, 8, 11, and 12; NCSS Standards IV, V, and VI

MATERIALS

✔ Tolan, S. (2002). *Surviving the Applewhites.* New York: HarperCollins. (one per student)

✔ CD: *The Sound of Music*

✔ Pondering Philosophy (page 76)

FEATURED READING COMPREHENSION STRATEGIES: Journal; Predict; Make Connections

Before Reading

JOURNAL

1. Ask students to respond to these questions as a journal entry: *What does it mean to survive? What kind of things do you currently do in order to survive? Are there different levels of survival? If so, what are they, and what level are you at?* Ask students to share their perspectives. Then collect their responses so they can reassess their perspectives after they finish reading the book.

PREDICT

2. Play the song "Climb Ev'ry Mountain" from *The Sound of Music* for the class. Ask students what they believe is the theme of this song. Ask them to predict why this song will be meaningful in this novel.

3. E.D. is not crazy about her given name—even if it does honor the great American writer Edith Wharton, someone whose work her mother clearly admires. Ask students if they know the stories about their names. If so, ask them share whether they like their names—or not (if the class did not do this activity previously with *Because of Winn-Dixie*).

During Reading

MAKE CONNECTIONS

1. In Chapter 3, as E.D. acknowledges that all of her older sister Cordelia's flower arrangements were beautiful: "She was a true Applewhite, after all, which meant that whatever creative activity she put her mind to, she did it really well" (p. 15). Ask students what makes them a "true *last name*."

2. In Chapter 9, E.D. says she feels invisible. Ask students why she says this. Is she really? Ask them if they have ever felt this way. Ask volunteers to recount their situation, explaining how it was similar to E.D.'s.

3. In Chapter 14, after Randolph decides that Jake will play the role of Rolf in *The Sound of Music*, Jake wonders whether he can act: "Something told him he could. Now that he thought about it, acting was what he'd been doing all his life" (p. 98). How so? Ask students to make "Jake's case."

```
              J
  r a diant light being
              k
radiant light being

              S
              e
              m
              p
 radiant  light being
              e
```

KEY BENEFIT

According to Howard Gardner (1973), honoring all the "intelligences"—for example, including music in the classroom—provides for more equitable, engaging, and enriching learning for every student.

After Reading

1. Ask students to use Jake's entire name, Jake Semple, to create an acrostic poem. Encourage them to find as many words as they can that other characters use to describe him in the book. They should write these words across the page, intersecting with the vertically written name on a common letter. The word does not have to begin with the common letter; for example, Lucille calls Jake a "radiant light being." As in the example (left) the phrase could be placed with the *a* in "Jake," or with either of the two *e's* in Semple. Students in small groups can review passages where Jake is described. They can create some adjectives themselves to complete the acrostic.

2. Play the recording of "Climb Ev'ry Mountain" again. Talk about how the message fits each of the Applewhites, Jeremy, and Govindaswami individually—and as a group. Then, discuss—and perhaps ask students to write about—Zedediah's question of Jake: "What gives you joy?" (p. 123).

3. Read aloud the opening paragraph of Chapter 29. Ask students to write about the "longest, most exhausting, most difficult day" of their lives.

4. Have students complete the Pondering Philosophy. Then, ask students what they think the theme(s) of the book is/are and which of the statements seem to support their perspective. Answers to page 76: 1. Grandfather/Zedediah Applewhite 2. Jake Semple 3. Randolph Applewhite 4. Applewhites 5. Zedediah 6. E.D. 7. Lucille 8. Randolph 9. Zedediah 10. Govindswami.

5. *Surviving the Applewhites* was chosen as a 2003 Newbery Honor Book. While only one book is named the Newbery winner each year, a number of honor books are also chosen. Have students write a review of the novel in which they explain whey they agree (or disagree) that this novel is worthy of this distinction.

Extension Activities

- Invite students to select one of the following topics that is mentioned in the novel to research. They can create a PowerPoint presentation, a poster, a bulletin board, or a demonstration to share what they learned; in other words, to design a "Teaching Opportunity," (p. 69) just like E.D. does for each of her curricular projects. Encourage students to determine what they believe the author's purpose was in including each of these references within her book—and why knowing a bit more about this is helpful to a reader:

* Edith Wharton (pp. 1, 68)	* A Midsummer's Night Dream (pp. 40, 126)	* Wyeths (p. 63)
* Galileo, Isaac Newton, Albert Einstein (p. 18)	* Reign of Terror (French Revolution) (p. 43)	* Barrymores (p. 64)
* Feng Shui (p. 24)		* Shakespeare (p. 68)
* Butterflies (p. 33)	* Hamlet (p. 58)	* Picasso (p. 68)
* Civil War (p. 40)	* Brontë sisters (p. 63)	* Meditation (p. 128)
		* Indian food (p. 142)

- Randolph believes that listening to loud music will make Jake deaf "before he's 20." Research this assertion and report findings to the class.

Further Reading

More books by Stephanie Tolan:
The Face in the Mirror. (1998). New York: Morrow Junior Books.
Flight of the Raven. (2001). New York: HarperCollins.
A Good Courage. (1998). New York: Beech Tree Books.
Listen. (2006). New York: HarperCollins.
Ordinary Miracles. (1999). New York: Morrow Junior Books.
Plague Year. (1999). New York: Beech Tree Books.
Welcome to the Ark. (2000). New York: Avon.

TECHNOLOGY LINKS

For more information about author Stephanie Tolan, visit:
http://www.stephanietolan.com
For more information about butterflies, visit these sites:
http://www.npwrc.usgs.gov/resource/distr/lepid/bflyusa/bflyusa.htm
http://www.butterflies.com
http://www.virtualmuseum.ca/Exhibitions/Butterflies/english/gallery/index.html

Cool Words Think Sheet

Audrey loves words! Can you tell what these words mean through their context and why Audrey would think they are cool? Be sure to rate each word!

1. I watched her snap the sheet and sail it deftly down.

"Frances? Can I ask you a personal question?"

She rolled her eyes. "Have I got a choice?"

"Do you hate working for white people?"

"Audrey Ina. The things that come out of your mouth."

"It is a **conundrum**," I agreed. (p. 26)

Conundrum means

_____

_____

5	4	3	2	1
coolest				not so cool

2. June was practically in tears. "I can't come to your house any more."

"How come?"

"She doesn't want me anywhere near you. She thinks something dangerous might happen."

"Oh, June, your mother's a **prodigious** worry-wart." (p. 100)

Prodigious means

_____

_____

5	4	3	2	1
coolest				not so cool

3. "Hey, Miss Farley. Hey, Tante." I gave my aunt a private smile of hello. She looked relieved to see me. "How was the bus?"

"Piece of cake," I replied. "Matter of fact, I had an **edifying** conversation with an old acquaintance of mine." (p. 126)

Edifying means

_____

_____

5	4	3	2	1
coolest				not so cool

4. So one fine night Tante joined me in the yard. A breeze played over the grass; katydids chirred their treetop **fandango**. (p. 166)

Fandango means

_____

_____

5	4	3	2	1
coolest				not so cool

_____ 's Cool Words

Find cool words of your own, from reading other books, magazines, newspapers, or billboards, or from the radio, television, CDs, movies, or even conversation. Write each word below. Why is it a cool word?

Cool word 1: _____

It's cool because _____

_____

Cool word 2: _____

It's cool because _____

_____

Cool word 3: _____

It's cool because _____

_____

Cool word 4: _____

It's cool because _____

_____

Cool word 5: _____

It's cool because _____

_____

Shiloh Think Sheet

Inference	Text Support	Page/Paragraph
The family lives in a rural area.		
They are not wealthy.		
Marty is compassionate toward animals.		
His father doesn't share his concern.		
Ma is a "typical" mother.		
Other		

Discussion Web

Should Marty have hidden Shiloh?

Yes

1. _____

2. _____

3. _____

No

1. _____

2. _____

3. _____

Our Final Decision:

Dear _____ Think Sheet

_____
(date)

Dear _____,

_____

_____

_____

_____

_____

_____

_____

_____

_____

_____

_____

_____

_____

_____

_____

_____,
(closing)

_____
(Your signature)

Pondering Philosophy

Tolan includes quite a bit of philosophy about life in this novel—ideas worthy of further consideration. Read each of the statements below, look them up so you can see each in context, discover which character made each statement, and then respond to each. Be ready to talk about how each contributes to the theme.

1. "More often than not, I've noticed, it [a rose-colored view of things] turns out to be true." (p. 4)

_____

_____

2. "Nobody could ever tell _____ that words didn't have power." (p. 7)

_____

3. Without creativity and individuality, there would be no scientific discovery. No Galileo, no

Newton, no Einstein." (p. 18) _____

_____

4. "Education is an adventurous quest for the meaning of life, involving an ability to think

things through." (p. 27) _____

5. "The most important thing you're going to learn while you're here is who you are and what

you're made of." (p. 37) _____

_____

6. We have "better things to do with our time" than watch TV. (p. 38) _____

_____

7. "Human beings are almost infinitely adaptable." (p. 40) _____

_____

8. "How sharper than a serpent's tooth is an ungrateful child!" (p. 77) _____

_____

9. "What gives you joy?" (p. 123) _____

_____

Chapter 4

Taking Action

How would you respond if you were confronted with a situation you found personally or socially intolerable? What if compliance was expected and powerfully enforced? What if those around you followed orders or conformed to the status quo without protest? Would apathy or fear compel you to do the same? Would your conscience, your resolve, perhaps even your stubbornness cause you to do something else?

History is replete with examples of heroes and heroines who opted to take a less traveled path, the one that was more difficult and often more dangerous, yet ultimately more rewarding. Some entered and exited history quietly. Others were propelled to instant and indelible fame or notoriety. Still others already had some measure of influence before they took the stand for which they are renowned. But all chose to seize the moment and they made a difference. These people changed lives and, in so doing, they changed themselves.

In this chapter, students will read works of fiction and nonfiction in which the main characters show no (or almost no) hesitation when taking action seems critical. Though the consequences are potentially serious, these people demonstrate that they are brave, compassionate, determined, prideful, headstrong, or all of these. Love them or hate them, there are no shrinking violets among this group!

The Children's Book of Heroes
edited by William Bennett

The Children's Book of Heroes is an edited volume of poems and prose that explore the idea of who is a "hero" and what qualities it takes to become one. This book is perfect for focusing on this topic as a theme study—or for "sampling," as class time permits. The editor of *The Children's Book of Heroes*, William Bennett, created this book because he wanted to help parents in their quest to provide suitable role models for their children. He believes that it "makes a big difference whether or not adults make efforts to point out what actions merit honor and which individuals deserve to be admired." Notice he says "adults," not just parents; teachers can use these selections, too. He believes that illustrator Michael Hague's "charming, magical paintings . . . speak to the hearts and imaginations of children. The combination of a few good stories, the illustrations, and a parent's (or teacher's) voice reading aloud is a great way to lift children's thoughts toward what is noble and fine." Indeed.

While the title of the book may say "children's," the stories are ageless and provide role models for people of all ages. Middle grade students are developmentally poised to "take action," but action is predicated on beliefs, whether implicitly or explicitly acknowledged. This text provides models across time, gender, and genre to help middle graders think about who they want to be and how those decisions will play out in their lives.

STANDARDS: IRA/NCTE Standards 1, 2, 3, 4, 5, 6, 11, and 12; NCSS Standards I, II, IV, V, and X

MATERIALS

✔ Bennett, W. (Ed.) (1997). *The Children's Book of Heroes*. New York: Simon & Schuster. (one per student)

✔ Analysis Think Sheet (page 94, one per student)

✔ Index cards (one per student)

FEATURED READING COMPREHENSION STRATEGIES: Quickwrite; Predict; Evaluate

Before Reading

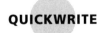

1. Ask students to list the names of up to three heroes, along with the qualities these people each have that make them heroes. Discuss students' answers as a class, making a master list of heroes and their defining characteristics.

2. Ask students to predict whether they will find their heroes and their characteristics in the selections they will read, and to explain why or why not. Next, read aloud William Bennett's introduction and discuss it with students. Once more, ask students to predict what heroes Bennett has included in this volume and why. Make a list as a class and then compare it with the topics in the book. Discuss why their choices may be different from Bennett's.

During Reading

1. As students read through the book, complete, as a class, the Analysis Think Sheet. This sheet encourages students to identify the different kinds of texts that Bennett has included. Be sure students understand what the three key genres are: poetry, fiction, and nonfiction. Second, help students to understand that because traditional literature originates from stories retold from generation to generation before being written down, these stories are classified as "oral history," and are thus located in the nonfiction area of the library. Point out, however, that most people consider these to be just stories, much like the fictional narratives Bennett also includes in this volume. The biographical sketches he includes are more typical nonfiction, information about real people that is accepted as factual.

2. Ask students to determine the genre of each selection and keep a record of each hero's characteristics on the Analysis Think Sheet.

Analysis Think Sheet

TITLE	CHARACTERISTICS OF A HERO	GENRE
Heroes		
Opportunity		
About Angels		
A Prayer at Valley Forge		
Only a Dad		
The Sphinx		
Jackie Robinson		
Sail On! Sail On!		
David and Goliath		
Our Heroes		
Honest Abe		
How the Animals Got Sunlight		
The Star Jewels		
Mother Teresa		
The Knights of the Silver Shield		
The Minotaur		
Helen Keller's Teacher		
Father Flanagan		
The Hero of Indian Cliff		
Tashira's Turn		
When Mother Reads Aloud		

After Reading

1. After discussing many or all of these selections, ask students to select and read a biography or autobiography of someone that they listed as a hero in the Before Reading activity or have come to think of as a hero from the reading. Then ask them to prepare an oral report for the class. It should include a brief summary of the person's life and highlight the actions that made her or him a hero.

KEY BENEFIT
Students who can identify the genre of the text they are reading better comprehend that text because they bring the appropriate background knowledge and motivation to the task.

2. Ask students to think of a hero "closer to home." Have them write the person a letter that explains why the person is a hero. Remind students to thank the person for being a significant influence in the student's life.

3. Ask students which of the selections was their favorite and why. Have them write the title of their favorite selection on the top line of an index card and a paragraph explaining why underneath. Then, ask them to write, in the upper-right corner, the genre of the selection, such as poetry, fiction, biography, myth/legend, pourquoi tale, or wonder/fairy tale. Help students find another selection of that same type. For example, if a student liked "How the Animals Got Sunlight," help her or him find another pourquoi tale, perhaps from *Pourquoi Tales: The Cat's Purr, Why Frog and Snake Never Play Together,* and *The Fire Bringer* by Ashley Bryan (1989, Houghton Mifflin School) or *When the World Was Young: Creation and Pourquoi Tales* by Margaret Mayo (1996, Simon & Schuster). After students have read another selection, ask them to create their own mini-poster with an illustration, along with a summary of the new story or a new poem.

EVALUATE

Extension Activities

• Create a class anthology of fiction, nonfiction, and poetry on a topic of interest, such as *The Children's Book of Egypt, The Children's Book of California, The Children's Book of the Revolutionary War,* or *The Children's Book of Mountains.*

79

Further Reading

Bennett, W. (1993). *The Book of Virtues*. New York: Simon & Schuster.
Bennett, W. (1998). *The Children's Book of America*. New York: Simon & Schuster.
Bennett, W. (1996). *The Children's Book of Virtues*. New York: Simon & Schuster.

TECHNOLOGY LINKS

For more information about heroism, visit these sites:

http://www.purpleheart.org

http://www.myhero.com

Captain Kate
by Carolyn Reeder

The year is 1864 and America is in the midst of the Civil War. When Kate Betts's bedridden mother informs her that their canal boat, on which the family depends for its livelihood, must be rented out to strangers for the coming season, the 12-year-old takes matters into her own hands.

Feeling betrayed both by her mother's rental plans and her recent remarriage, Kate resolves to prove that she herself is fully capable of captaining the boat her beloved father had piloted before his death. Goading her new stepbrother, Seth, into accompanying her, Kate sets out from Cumberland, Maryland, to deliver coal in Washington, D.C. Dressed as a boy and filled with determination and attitude, she strives to show Seth she is superior to him in every way. On her voyage down the canal, however, she learns much more than how to captain a boat. She learns to face her fears, let go of the past, and appreciate the present.

Though the focus of this novel is on Kate's achievement and her relationship with her new family, its historical context makes it a good choice for pairing with a study of the Civil War. In a developmental stage where they are beginning to yearn for autonomy, middle schoolers will admire Kate's spunk and self-sufficiency. Many will also be bothered by her bossiness and downright meanness toward her stepbrother, behavior which may offer students dealing with blended families something to ponder.

STANDARDS: IRA/NCTE STANDARDS: 1, 2, 3, 5, 6, 7, 8, 9, 11, and 12; NCSS Standards I, III, and IV

MATERIALS

✔ Reeder, C. (1999). *Captain Kate*. New York: Avon Books. (one per student)

✔ Overhead transparencies with historic photos of C & O Canal and Photo Analysis Worksheet available through the National Park Service's Web site:

❏ family on canal boat	❏ canal boat	❏ canal locks
❏ Paw Paw Tunnel	❏ canal boats unloading coal	

✔ Map of C & O Canal route

✔ Photo, diagram, or model of a canal boat (see the National Canal Museum's Web site)

✔ Drawing paper and markers or colored pencils.

FEATURED READING COMPREHENSION STRATEGIES: Background Knowledge;
Visualize; Graphic Organizer: Character Web

Before Reading

1. To generate interest in the novel and build background knowledge, display on an overhead projector the transparency depicting family life on a canal boat. Distribute the Photo Analysis Worksheet and have students pair up to complete the questions. They should notice the children, their dress, the chains securing them for safety reasons, a woman who is apparently their mother, and the background. Encourage students to use these clues to speculate about the photo's setting, time, and place. If students have difficulty, prompt them with questions: *Why might the children be chained? Do they look distressed? In what sorts of places might such restraints be necessary?* Display the next transparency of a canal boat and scaffold as necessary to help students infer that the children in the first photo are secured to the roof of one of these vessels.

2. Introduce the novel. The cover illustration presents another opportunity to discuss the boats: *When were they used? Where? For what purposes? What do you know about rivers that might explain the advent of the canal system?* Supplement the study of *Captain Kate* with books and Internet articles about canals as necessary to further students' knowledge.

BACKGROUND KNOWLEDGE

During Reading

1. After students read the first three chapters, encourage them to voice their initial opinions about Kate's decision to take the boat down the waterway without her mother's permission. Speculate about the obstacles or dangers she may encounter.

2. Display the map of the C & O canal route. Ask students to explain its location in relation to the river and towpath. To clarify, read aloud passages from the book that describe the canal, stopping intermittently to think aloud as you quickly sketch your vision of the canal's layout. Invite students to provide input and sketch along. Afterward, display your sketch and add to it as other terms (for example, berm, lock, snubbing post, aqueduct) are introduced.

KEY BENEFIT

This process encourages students to attend to visual clues and use them to draw inferences, a higher-level thinking skill imperative for good comprehension. Proficient readers visualize the text as they read. Teacher modeling illustrates the process. This strategy also engages visual and kinesthetic learners.

3. Next, have students create a labeled diagram of the boat's configuration from Kate's description of its dimensions and components: tiller, bow, stern, hatches, cabin, pump well, mule stable, race plank, etc. Afterward, display a canal boat photo or diagram and have students analyze it and make corrections and adjustments to their own drawings. This activity will increase students' understanding of the novel and enhance their awareness of diagrams as comprehension tools.

VISUALIZE

4. Show the remaining transparencies as they coincide with the action in the story. For example, display the photo of Paw Paw Tunnel and talk about it before reading Chapter Ten. Link to students' backgrounds: *Have you ever traveled through a long tunnel? What was it like? Why might people be afraid? How would traversing the tunnel*

in a canal boat differ from being in a car or train? Discuss Kate's fear of the tunnel and how she copes with it on the initial and return trips.

5. Have students consider how Kate treats Seth. *Why is she so resentful? What do her actions say about her? At what points in the novel does Seth assert himself and take pivotal actions of his own? What can we determine about him based on his behavior?*

After Reading

1. Revisit Kate's reasons for disregarding her mother's wishes and embarking on the canal trip. Ask: *Regarding Kate's actions, do the ends justify the means? What has Kate learned?*

2. Have each student choose one of the novel's main characters—Kate, Seth, Zeke, or Julia—to analyze. Guide students in creating webs on which they identify their character's traits, along with specific behaviors that reveal these qualities. Page numbers may be added so students can look back for discussion purposes. A web of Zeke's character and actions may look like the following example:

Understands what you tell him:
- Plays his harmonica when Kate asks.
- Follows instructions to load mules, tie up, wash cabin, etc.
- Stays in cabin when Kate orders him to.

Does the work of a man:
- Sleeps in the hay house by himself.
- Takes each day's last shift driving mules.
- Works in the dark and rain.

ZEKE

Thinks like a child:
- Stays in cabin as ordered, even when it fills with smoke.
- Chooses inappropriate way to stand up for himself (dangles young boy over water).

Good and kind:
- Sympathizes with injured Rebel.
- Never criticizes Kate or Seth.
- Does least desirable jobs without complaint.
- Always willing to help.

Finally, instruct students to use their webs to create diary entries in the voice of the character they've analyzed. For example, a student may assume the role of Kate and write a diary entry in which she talks about Zeke and his contributions as a crew member.

Extension Activities

- Once students read the information at the end of the book on the C & O Canal, they can investigate:
  - ❏ its full name (Chesapeake and Ohio) and the purposes it served
  - ❏ its significance to the Union and the Confederacy during the Civil War
  - ❏ its demise (trains were more efficient; floods destroyed the canal)
  - ❏ historic accounts of incidents on the canal.

- Students can visit the National Canal Museum online and take a virtual tour.

- Invite students to find examples of other women in history who took action and, through their unconventional roles, made important contributions: Harriet Tubman, Sojourner Truth, Susan B. Anthony, Sacagawea, Clara Barton, Amelia Earhart, and Rosa Parks are just a few possibilities.

Further Reading

Harness, C. (1995). *The Amazing Impossible Erie Canal*. New York: Aladdin Paperbacks.

Reit, S. (1991). *Behind Enemy Lines: The Incredible Story of Emma Edmonds, Civil War Spy*. New York: Harcourt Young Classics.

Rinaldi, A. (2001). *Girl in Blue*. New York: Scholastic.

TECHNOLOGY LINKS

Canals: http://xroads.virginia.edu/~MA98/haven/transport/canal.html

The National Canal Museum: http://www.canals.org/ncm/

The National Park Service: http://www.cr.nps.gov/nr/twhp/wwwlps/lessons/10cando/10cando.htm

Hoot

by Carl Hiaasen

What do a school bully, a runaway boy, a pancake restaurant, a hapless police officer, a frustrated construction foreman, and a bunch of endangered owls have to do with Roy Eberhardt, the new kid at Trace Middle School? Plenty, if Carl Hiaasen is their creator. A columnist for the *Miami Herald* and author of several adult novels, Hiaasen has brought to life a colorful set of characters in this 2003 Newbery Honor Book, his first for adolescents.

When his father is transferred yet again, Roy reluctantly leaves the mountains of Bozeman, Montana, for Coconut Cove, Florida. He has come to expect the initiation he invariably experiences at each new school: eating lunch by himself, trying to establish a network of friends, and enduring the physical torment inflicted on him by the ever present school bully. What he doesn't anticipate, however, is an intriguing mystery that unfolds when, from the bus window, he spots a shoeless, bookless boy sprinting away from the school. Making it his mission to learn the runaway's identity, Roy eventually uncovers the truth: "Mullet Fingers" is sabotaging the construction site where Mother Paula's All-American Pancake House is attempting to build its newest restaurant. The reason: A colony of burrowing owls is nesting on the land. In the end, Roy joins Mullet Fingers in taking a stand for the environment and against corporate greed.

Hiaasen, in demonstrating that young people can make a difference, relays his message through an appealingly funny story with memorable characters and witty dialogue. With irreverent humor that middle schoolers will appreciate, it is a good choice for independent reading followed by small- or whole-group discussion.

STANDARDS: IRA/NCTE STANDARDS: 1, 2, 3, 4, 5, 6, 7, 11, and 12; NCSS Standards III, IV, and VI

MATERIALS

✔ Hiaasen, C. (2002). *Hoot*. New York: Knopf. (one per student)

✔ Copy of the *Miami Herald* (containing Hiaasen's biweekly column)

❑ Copies of Hiaasen's column (one per student)

❑ A list of the *Herald*'s columnists (on a transparency)

❑ Handout bearing the titles of Hiaasen's recent columns (one per student)
(All are available through the *Herald*'s Web site.)

✔ Dictionary

✔ Construction paper or oaktag covers for journals

✔ Journal pages with owl eyes

✔ Stapler, markers, and other materials for assembling journals

FEATURED READING COMPREHENSION STRATEGIES: Background Knowledge; Infer; Journal; Determine Importance

Before Reading

1. Distribute the book and encourage students to comment on its unique cover and title, both of which should arouse curiosity and hypotheses about the story. Ask if anyone has ever heard of the author.

2. Display a copy of the *Miami Herald*, pointing out that, like all major newspapers, it employs dozens of columnists. Discuss what a columnist does. Then, display the transparency with the names of the *Herald*'s columnists. Ask students to inspect the list, noting the categories (news, editorial, sports, business, etc.) and checking to see if any of the names look familiar. They should see Hiaasen's name under "Editorial Columnists." (Note: Some may recognize Dave Barry's name, as well, who is one of the Living section columnists for the newspaper.) Ask them to speculate about the differences in the types of columns. A sports or technology columnist's focus is pretty clear, but what about editorial columnists? What do they write about? Scaffold students' understanding by asking one of them to locate the words *editorial* and *editorialize* in a dictionary and read their meanings aloud.

BACKGROUND KNOWLEDGE

INFER

3. Distribute copies of Hiaasen's *Herald* column, as well as the handouts with the titles of his recent columns. Divide students into pairs or small groups and give them five to ten minutes to scan them. Their task should be to determine whether there are any common threads running through Hiaasen's writing. Each group should record its thoughts about his editorial focus (the environment, political corruption, injustice, etc.) and then share them with the entire class.

4. Discuss Hiaasen's dual career as an editorial columnist and a novelist. Finally, pose this question: *Knowing what you now do about the author and his editorial writing, can you speculate more accurately about his interests and the book's content?*

During Reading

Use a literature circle format for reading the novel:

1. Determine the length of time you will allot to the study of the book. Divide the class into groups of four or five and tell them they will be reading the majority of the book outside of class. Establish a completion date and announce that each group will be setting its own reading schedule. Add that they will be given regular class time to discuss the novel in their circles.

2. Have students construct and decorate journal covers out of construction paper or oaktag. Distribute journal pages—sheets of paper on which you've printed owl eyes similar to those on the book's face—and have students staple the pages to their covers.

JOURNAL

3. Tell students they are to use the journal pages to jot down points of interest they see as they read (hence, the "eyes"). Read aloud a few passages and model your own thought processes as you read, making note of personal connections, opinions, predictions, and so on. Allot 20 to 30 minutes of in-class time for students to begin silently reading Chapter 1 and recording a few thoughts and observations.

Tip: Use a "fishbowl" format to demonstrate appropriate discussion techniques: Sit with one group of students in front of the class, encouraging members to share their initial written observations and discuss the story as the other students observe. Model suitable discussion questions, responses, and so on. Afterward, hold a whole-class exchange on the discussion. Make sure students understand the expectations for courteous, productive group behaviors.

---

4. Each group should meet and determine how many pages they will read for their first literature circle discussion. In preparation, each student should do the following: (a) Identify the date and portion of text read; (b) record five observations about the reading, for example, predictions, opinions about characters and events; (c) mark a favorite passage with a sticky-note and be prepared to read it aloud, explaining why the student selected it; and (c) write a question or provocative statement related to the story the student would like to discuss with the group. If desired, roles such as recorder, illustrator, and vocabulary word finder can be rotated among group members.

5. Set aside class time (15 to 30 minutes) for regular literature circle discussions as the novel is read. Circulate among groups as they share their journals and discuss the novel. Play the role of observer, allowing students to maintain control of their discussions and prompting them only if necessary to enhance or redirect the conversations. Assess students on their preparedness, group contributions, and behavior.

KEY BENEFIT

In a literature circle, students in small groups take leadership in discussing a text. Instead of teacher-centered instruction, students first read and respond to a book individually, and then they share their observations with their classmates. Because ownership is motivating, literature circles typically work well.

After Reading

DETERMINE IMPORTANCE

1. Focus students on the "taking action" aspects of the story: Ask: *What motives do you think drove Roy to get involved with Mullet Fingers and his sister, Beatrice? What specific actions did he take that escalated his role in preventing the construction of the pancake restaurant? What do you think he learned in the process?* Give students a blank flow chart, on which they should identify actions they consider significant. Students' choices may vary. What is important is that they are able to justify them in a follow-up discussion.

2. Ensure that students spend time either in small or large groups discussing bullying, a significant issue in this story and in nearly every school. Ask them to evaluate how Roy handles his nemesis, Dana Matherson: *What actions did he take to deal with Dana? Were they effective? Appropriate? What is the best course of action if you are a victim of bullying? What should you do if you witness a bullying incident? In general, how should students, school personnel, and parents handle this problematic behavior?* Have students visit the Web sites of the American Academy of Child and Adolescent Psychiatry or the National Education Association's Bullying Awareness Campaign for a more in-depth look at this pervasive problem.

3. Revisit the topic of the author's career and personal interests. Ask: *In retrospect, how does the book reflect Hiaasen's personal concerns? Is he trying to convey a message?*

Extension Activities

- Invite students to scout newspapers and magazines for examples of people taking action on issues important to them. Have them bring the articles to class in order to discuss the worthiness of the causes and the appropriateness of the actions.

- Encourage students to search the Internet for more information on burrowing owls and other endangered species. Display photos and relevant information they find on a class bulletin board. As a class, write letters to newspaper editors or to government officials supporting the protection of these species.

- Students can research environmental groups and find out how they are working to protect the environment. Help students initiate an environmental project of their choice.

Further Reading

Bauer, J. (2002). *Hope Was Here*. New York: Puffin.

Konigsburg, E. L. (2004). *The Outcasts of 19 Schuyler Place*. New York: Atheneum.

TECHNOLOGY LINKS

The American Academy of Child and Adolescent Psychiatry:
   http://www.aacap.org/publications/factsfam/80.htm

The National Education Association: http://www.nea.org/schoolsafety/bullying.html

For information about Carl Hiaasen:
   http://www.miami.com/mld/miamiherald/news/columnists/

To locate information about burrowing owls and other endangered animals, visit:
   National Geographic's Creature Feature:
   http://www.nationalgeographic.com/kids/creature_feature/0102/orangutans.html
   The Owl Pages: http://www.owlpages.com/species/gallery.html
   The U. S. Fish and Wildlife Service: http://endangered.fws.gov
   Wildlife Trust: http://www.wildlifetrust.org

Flying Solo

by Ralph Fletcher

Is flying solo preferable to being supervised? How do we and our students prefer to "fly" through life?

Sixth grader Rachel has chosen not to say a word since her classmate died unexpectedly the previous school year. While watching a detective show, she heard, "You have the right to remain silent." As the novel begins, she has already chosen to exercise that right for six months.

The novel is told as a time line, primarily of one school day, although the book actually spans four days. What would happen if a substitute teacher did not come to class—and none of the school authorities realized it? What if the sixth-grade class decided to run their own classroom for a day? What might happen? Middle schoolers believe they are ready to take over the world—at least their corner of it. This compelling novel provides middle graders with a realistic (although not probable) situation to think about their readiness to do just that.

STANDARDS: IRA/NCTE Standards: 1, 3, 4, 5, 6, 7, 8, 11, and 12; NCSS Standards IV, V, VI, and X

MATERIALS

✔ Fletcher, R. (1998). *Flying Solo*. New York: Clarion. (one per student)

✔ CD of Tchaikovsky's *1812 Overture* or of the Counting Crows

✔ Viorst, J. (1972) *Alexander and the Terrible, Horrible, No Good, Very Bad Day*. New York: Atheneum.

✔ Fact and Opinion Think Sheet (page 95, one per student)

FEATURED READING COMPREHENSION STRATEGIES: Journal; Text-to-Self Connections; Evaluate; Analyze Fact and Opinion

Before Reading

1. Ask students to respond to these questions as a journal entry:

   - *What does it mean to "fly solo"?*

   - *When would it be a good thing for middle-school students to do?*

   - *When would it be risky for a middle-school student to do?*

   - *When would it be absolutely unwise for a middle schooler to "fly solo"?*

   - *Why do you think Fletcher chose this title for the novel?*

   Ask students to share their perspectives and then collect their responses so that students can reassess their perspectives after they finish reading the book.

KEY BENEFIT
Responding to specific questions in journals before reading gives students a chance to record what they currently think about a topic before being influenced by peers or the text they will read. They then have a reference point if their thinking or understanding changes over time.

JOURNAL

2. Let students know that as they read the novel, they should consider the criteria for stories that Mr. Fabiano has listed on his wall. Tell them that after they have finished reading the novel, you will ask them to rate the success of this story on these criteria.

Stories . . .

1. are unique as snowflakes. No two are exactly alike.

2. contain small details that often turn out to be important.

3. involve limits; particular characters in a particular place and time.

4. put characters in difficult situations.

5. force characters to make moral choices.

6. contain a problem or conflict that often gets worse before it gets better.

7. connect the ordinary with the extraordinary.

8. usually contain a surprise or two.

9. sometimes turn on a "moment of silence."

10. rarely turn out the way you expect. (p. 46)

During Reading

1. Karen makes an "executive decision" when she delivers the lunch count and attendance sheet to the office without revealing that the substitute teacher has not reported to her class. When she tells her classmates that the office doesn't know because she didn't tell them, her classmates both agree and disagree with her decision. As a class, begin the creation of a chart of who agrees and disagrees with Karen's decision, and their rationale. Continue recording students' perceptions throughout the reading of the text.

2. At 9:50, Mr. Fabiano's class participates in Flashdrafts, sustained silent writing with background music designed to set an appropriate mood for writing. Before reading this section to the class, ask students to write for 20 minutes with music playing softly in the background, perhaps something by Counting Crows or the *1812 Overture*. Provide time for sharing, to complete Mr. Fabiano's ritual.

3. The "Rock Ritual" has the potential to be the most dramatic of all the rituals in which the students participate since it allows class members to say good-bye to a classmate. Ask students why they think it didn't work when Mr. Fabiano's class tried to do it after Tommy died. Discuss whether it went well when they tried to do it for Bastian. Why or why not?

TEXT-TO-SELF CONNECTIONS
4. When Sean writes about Barkley "sleeping curled up on my bed," he says, "I got a feeling like Christmas morning" (p. 136). Ask students to write about a time they "got a feeling like Christmas morning."

After Reading

1. Ask students to design a new ritual for their classroom. What kind of ritual would help the class become more of a learning community? Ask students to include all of these sections in their "Ritual Proposal": the name of the ritual, the purpose of the ritual, the materials needed for it to occur, when it would occur (if not clear from the purpose), how it would occur, and the anticipated results.

2. Bastian writes about his "Terrible, Horrible No Good Day." Read Judith Viorst's picture book *Alexander and the Terrible, Horrible, No Good, Very Bad Day*. Then ask students to write about such a day they had: "*Student's name* and the Terrible, Horrible, No Good, Very Bad Day."

3. Ask students to rate the criteria you mentioned before reading (see page 87). They should use a plus (+) or a minus (–), depending on how well they believe this novel fulfills these criteria. Ask them to explain their rating.

EVALUATE

4. Ask students to complete the Fact and Opinion Think Sheet. They should discuss the definitions and examples. Then provide time for students to write their own examples, perhaps in small groups or with a partner first, and then individually. Provide time for students to share their sentences and explain them.

5. Ask students to reread their journal entries in response to the questions from the Before Reading activity, and then review the chart created in the second activity in the During Reading section. As a class, discuss the idea of taking action. Should Karen have told the office that there was no "responsible adult" in their classroom? If she didn't, should someone else have done so? Were the actions that students took during the day responsible? Can "students rule" safely? After an extensive discussion, ask students to address this issue by writing short essays. They should state their opinions but support them with evidence from the novel.

Fact and Opinion Think Sheet

Christopher is constantly analyzing what people say by labeling their thoughts as "fact" or "opinion." When Jessica notices that the class is to have a sub, Christopher says, "Fact." When Christopher is singing, "You make me Hap-peee . . . when skies are grayyyyy," Bastian says, "Not funny." Christopher's reponse? "Opinion."

What is the difference between fact and opinion?

Write the definitions of each.

Fact: _____

Opinion: _____

Read each of the following statements. Label them either "fact" or "opinion."

_____ One of the characters in this book was named Sean.

_____ Sean O'Day was shy.

_____ Rachel was foolish for not talking for six months.

_____ The Birthday Ritual included Mr. Fabiano's reading of *On the Day You Were Born*.

_____ When Karen went to the office to turn in the attendance report, she should have told the secretary that the substitute teacher had not shown up.

_____ Bastian did the right thing when he gave his puppy to Sean.

_____ Bastian gave his puppy to Sean.

_____ *Flying Solo* is the best book Ralph Fletcher has ever written.

_____ *Flying Solo* is one of many books Ralph Fletcher has written.

Write four statements, two that are facts and two that are opinions.

Fact: _____

Opinion: _____

Extension Activities

- Have students create a map that shows all of the Air Force bases where Bastian and his parents lived. Then, in small groups, students should research two of the bases and create a Venn diagram to compare and contrast them.

- In small groups, students can prepare a report on any of the pilots Rachel thinks about at the beginning of the book: Amelia Earhart, Charles Lindbergh, Sally Ride, or John Glenn. If more famous aviators are needed, you may want to suggest Orville and Wilbur Wright, Neil Armstrong, and Bessie Coleman.

- Bastian is moving to Hawaii. Invite small groups of students to research one of the following categories concerning the newest state: history, natural features, agriculture, industry, and tourist attractions. Each group should create a tri-fold board to display.

- Ask for volunteers to choose another of Fletcher's books to read, and then present a book talk to the class.

Further Reading

Other works by Ralph Fletcher:

NOVELS

Fig Pudding. (1996). New York: Yearling.
Spider Boy. (1998). New York: Yearling.

POEMS
Have You Been to the Beach Lately?: Poems. (2001). New York: HarperCollins.
Ordinary Things: Poems from a Walk in Early Spring. (1997). New York: Atheneum.
Relatively Speaking. (2001). New York: HarperCollins.

TECHNOLOGY LINKS
For more information about author Ralph Fletcher, visit these sites:
    http://www.ralphfletcher.com
For more information about flight, visit these sites:
    http://www.museumofflight.org
    http://www.flight-history.com
    http://www.centennialofflight.gov/index.cfm

Burning Up

by Caroline B. Cooney

Caroline B. Cooney's *Burning Up* is an ideal novel for a unit called "Taking Action." Its realistic plot, romantic interludes, and significant social commentary make it a compelling story and one that will really engage middle schoolers.

Fifteen-year-old Macey Clare has always loved living in her quiet, Connecticut hometown. Required to do a history project for school, Macey begins to research a fire that took place in 1959 in the barn across the street from her grandparents' house. Her initial questions spawn more questions, because even the few answers she obtains seem to indicate it was a racial incident.

This theme plays out in this significant—but not preachy—novel. Particularly for schools where service learning or character education are key components of the curriculum, this book would be particularly appropriate.

STANDARDS: IRA/NCTE Standards 1, 2, 3, 4, 5, 6, 7, 8, 9, 11, and 12; NCSS Standards I, II, III, IV, V, VI, and X

MATERIALS

✔ Cooney, C. B. (2001). *Burning Up.* New York: Laurel-Leaf. (one per student)

✔ Symbolism Think Sheet (page 96, one per student)

FEATURED READING COMPREHENSION STRATEGIES: Journal; Make Connections, Analyze Symbolism

Before Reading

1. Before students have even seen the cover of the book, ask them to think about these questions: *What does another person's suffering have to do with me? And what can I do about it?* Have them respond in a journal entry. Collect and save their responses for a comparison activity once the novel has been read.

2. Ask students to think about the book's title. What possibilities for "burning up" come to their minds? Record their answers on an overhead transparency. Then, show them the book's cover and ask them to again predict what they think the focus of the novel may be, refining or adding to their original ideas. Keep the transparency for future reference.

MAKE CONNECTIONS

3. Ask students if they have ever participated in a community service event, such things as collecting items for food pantries or walking, running, or even jumping rope to raise money for worthwhile causes. Ask them why they participated—and how it felt. If students haven't participated, ask them why not. Talk about the kinds of people who benefit from such activities, especially among the participants—not just the recipients.

During Reading

1. On page 2, Cooney says, "Macey was not basically a sitting-down person, but she loved to sit here." What does such a statement tell the reader about Macey? Discuss with the class. Then, if desired, use the frame of that statement to invite students to write about themselves. Ask them to fill in the blanks:
" _____ *student's name* was not basically a _____ person, but he/she loved to _____ here." Then, students would explain their statement.

For example, a student named Sarah may write:

> Sarah was not basically a patient person, but she loved to be infinitely patient here. Her garden brought out her most careful and deliberate actions. She loved the methodical work of marking the spaces where she would first create holes. She craved the feeling of the sun-warmed soil between her fingers as she made the nests for the waiting seedlings. She felt expectant as she cradled each young plant into the holes, and then gently covered the roots with a blanket of earth. Indeed, patience was a virtue, as Sarah's mother always said. Indeed, only patience, along with a little sun and a little water, would nurture the burgeoning life within each stem.

2. Fire is a symbol used throughout the book; silence becomes more than silence; even crayons become symbolic. Ask students to make notes as they read on the Symbolism Think Sheet. Whenever these things or qualities are mentioned, they should be sure to note the page number. Also, ask them to be on the lookout for other items or instances that seem to have more significance than they normally would and note these at the bottom of the page. Discuss the growing lists as students read through the chapters.

Symbolism Think Sheet

For Macey, the fire that occurs when she and her friends are painting the Sunday school room at the church becomes a symbol for the fire "burning" within her to find the truth. Where else are fires featured in the novel? As you read the novel, make notes here each time fire is mentioned. Be sure to include the page number.

_____
_____
_____

The crayons in the Sunday school rooms: What might these childhood objects represent? As you read the novel, take notes each time crayons occurs in the text.

_____
_____
_____

The silence of Macey's and Austin's grandparents, Macey's and Austin's parents, the townspeople: What might the silence represent? As you read the novel, take notes each time Macey and/or Austin do not get much information from those they question.

_____
_____
_____

How do these symbols contribute to the theme(s) of this novel?

_____
_____

Are there any other items that seem to hold more than their apparent meaning?

_____ : _____
_____ : _____

For example, the first of the seasonal bonfires on the beach is mentioned on page 5. On page 9, Macey mentions the barn's burning—and the pause in the conversation with her grandparents that follows. On page 25, Macey notices the state of the crayons that have been sent for the children in the after-school program at Good Shepherd church. Once students have finished reading the book, ask them to choose one item and write about it. They should be sure to write a topic sentence that explains the meaning of the symbol, and to use specific instances, taken from the notes on the Think Sheet to support their conclusion.

3. The idea of justice is a constant theme in the book. Ask students to keep a two-column chart. They should list each time the idea of fairness or justice occurs in the text. Explain to students that those words may not be used in the text but that the concept is there just the same. Ask students to write the quote and the page number in the left-hand column and comment on why they chose that quote and how that quote speaks to them of fairness or justice in the right-hand column. For example, a student may choose this excerpt about the character Austin: "Now he stared into his soul, the one that thought he deserved better than Venita and Davonn and Chamique and Isaiah, and that didn't get him anywhere either." The student's commentary may be: "How arrogant Austin is! Why should he deserve more than Venita, Davonn, Chamique, and Isaiah? He should deserve more just because he's white? Instead of black? He's wrong. Absolutely wrong."

4. Mrs. Framm tells Macey that "Mr. Sibley changed Bonnie's life. She became a Freedom Rider in the sixties because of Mr. Sibley. He was the first black person she ever met, and the best teacher she ever had, and she decided to teach high-school chemistry in his honor" (p. 120). Ask students to answer this question: *What is a Freedom Rider?* Have them use the Web sites in the Technology Links section or other reference materials to create a profile of someone who was a Freedom Rider.

After Reading

1. Ask students to reread their notes about symbolism and ask them to discuss: *How do these symbols, as a whole, contribute to the theme(s) of this novel?* Then, ask them to share any additional symbols they noted as they were reading through the novel. As a class, come to a consensus on whether these items are symbolic.

2. Have students consider once again the questions: *What does another person's suffering have to do with me? And what can I do about it?* Ask them to respond, once again, in a journal entry. Then, pass back their original responses. Give them a chance to reread what they wrote initially. Encourage them to see whether their answers changed, and if so, in what way, from before they read the book. Ask them if this activity encourages them to take action.

3. What is the message—and more important—the plan of action that Macey would want readers to undertake? Support the class in designing and implementing some kind of service project—to show their true colors.

Extension Activities

- Shakespeare's *Hamlet* was the play that Venita was all "fired up" about reading in school. Students can read it in its entirety either online at http://thetech.mit.edu/Shakespeare/hamlet/. Interested groups of students could select a scene to present to the class, explaining why or why not it might have been a favorite of Venita.

- Students who are really interested in the author, can read her biography, *Caroline Cooney: Faith and Fiction* by Pamela Sissi Carroll (Scarecrow Press, 2002). Have these students present a book talk to the class.

Further Reading

More books by Caroline B. Cooney:

Code Orange. (2005). New York: Bantam Doubleday Dell.

Driver's Ed. (1996). New York: Laurel-Leaf.

The Face on the Milk Carton. (1991). New York: Laurel-Leaf.

The Girl Who Invented Romance. (2005). New York: Random House.

Goddess of Yesterday. (2002). New York: Delacorte.

The Ransom of Mercy Carter. (2002). New York: Laurel-Leaf.

The Voice on the Radio. (1998). New York: Laurel-Leaf.

What Janie Found. (2002). New York: Laurel-Leaf.

Whatever Happened to Janie? (1994). New York: Laurel-Leaf.

TECHNOLOGY LINKS

For more information about author Caroline B. Cooney, visit these sites:

    http://www.teenreads.com/authors/au-cooney-caroline.asp

    http://www.bookpage.com/9611bp/childrens/thevoiceontheradio.html

    http://www.scholastic.com/titles/authors/cooney/

For more information about Freedom Riders, visit these sites:

    http://www.watson.org/~lisa/blackhistory/civilrights-55-65/freeride.html

    http://www.freedomridersfoundation.org

Analysis Think Sheet

TITLE	CHARACTERISTICS OF A HERO	GENRE
Heroes		
Opportunity		
About Angels		
A Prayer at Valley Forge		
Only a Dad		
The Sphinx		
Jackie Robinson		
Sail On! Sail On!		
David and Goliath		
Our Heroes		
Honest Abe		
How the Animals Got Sunlight		
The Star Jewels		
Mother Teresa		
The Knights of the Silver Shield		
The Minotaur		
Helen Keller's Teacher		
Father Flanagan		
The Hero of Indian Cliff		
Tashira's Turn		
When Mother Reads Aloud		

Fact and Opinion Think Sheet

Christopher is constantly analyzing what people say by labeling their thoughts as "fact" or "opinion." When Jessica notices that the class is to have a sub, Christopher says, "Fact." When Christopher is singing, "You make me Hap-peee . . . when skies are grayyyyy," Bastian says, "Not funny." Christopher's response? "Opinion."

What is the difference between fact and opinion?

Write the definitions of each.

Fact: _____

Opinion: _____

Read each of the following statements. Label them either "fact" or "opinion."

_____ One of the characters in this book was named Sean.

_____ Sean O'Day was shy.

_____ Rachel was foolish for not talking for six months.

_____ The Birthday Ritual included Mr. Fabiano's reading of *On the Day You Were Born*.

_____ When Karen went to the office to turn in the attendance report, she should have told the secretary that the substitute teacher had not shown up.

_____ Bastian did the right thing when he gave his puppy to Sean.

_____ Bastian gave his puppy to Sean.

_____ *Flying Solo* is the best book Ralph Fletcher has ever written.

_____ *Flying Solo* is one of many books Ralph Fletcher has written.

Write four statements, two that are facts and two that are opinions.

Fact: _____

_____

Opinion: _____

_____

Symbolism Think Sheet

For Macey, the fire that occurs when she and her friends are painting the Sunday school room at the church becomes a symbol for the fire "burning" within her to find the truth. Where else are fires featured in the novel? As you read the novel, make notes here each time fire is mentioned. Be sure to include the page number.

_____

_____

_____

_____

The crayons in the Sunday school rooms: What might these childhood objects represent? As you read the novel, take notes each time crayons occurs in the text.

_____

_____

_____

The silence of Macey's and Austin's grandparents, Macey's and Austin's parents, the townspeople: What might the silence represent? As you read the novel, take notes each time Macey and/or Austin do not get much information from those they question.

_____

_____

_____

How do these symbols contribute to the theme(s) of this novel?

_____

_____

_____

Are there any other items that seem to hold more than their apparent meaning?

_____ : _____

_____ : _____

_____ : _____

Chapter 5

Immigration

Many adolescents have had the dreaded experience of moving from one school to another and assuming, at least temporarily, that most terrifying of identities: the "new kid." Relatively few, however, have moved from one country to another and faced the multiple challenges that confront immigrants. These newcomers regularly tackle the formidable task of trying to define themselves in a society that is often indifferent, unsympathetic, or even hostile to the unique languages and customs they bring with them. The herd mentality that characterizes adolescence dictates that distinctive characteristics—whether they involve physical appearance, intellectual ability, economic status, or other personal traits—be minimized in favor of the broader goal of "fitting in." More than nearly anything else, adolescents fear being different, and perhaps for this reason, they often ridicule differences in others.

The books in this chapter will introduce students to historical and contemporary immigrants, both fictional and real. Though their cultures may be unfamiliar, the human characteristics they display will be immediately recognizable: "I've felt like that before," students will think—and, perhaps, either proudly or regretfully, "I've acted like that before." When maximizing the teachable moments inspired by these books. you will be supporting the National Middle School Association's (2003) vision of "healthy school environments" where "human relationships are paramount" (p. 12).

Who Belongs Here?
by Margy Burns Knight

This picture book/nonfiction text is an ideal point to begin a unit on immigration. Students, reading newspaper headlines, might believe that immigration is only a contemporary issue. It is not. Except for Native Americans, whose ancestors inhabited this land before the earliest European explorers, Americans are the descendants of immigrants. It was in the early 20th century that America's population swelled with immigrants from both Europe and Asia. While students typically learn about European immigration—the story of people crossing the Atlantic to get to the East coast, particularly through the gateway known as Ellis Island—there are myriad stories of Japanese or Chinese immigrants who came through Angel Island, just outside San Francisco. In recent generations, immigrants from Mexico, Central America, South America, Africa, and Asia have also contributed to the overall story of immigration in the United States.

What do most of these stories have in common? Why did nearly all these people come to the United States? They desired a better life. America has traditionally been called "the land of opportunity." And it still is, as in the case of Nary, the main character in this unusual book. Throughout most of the book, the top part of the page recounts Nary's story, which is based on the recent history of Cambodia. The text on the bottom part of the page, printed in italics, provides background knowledge for the reader. The book can be read in layers. Reading the top layer first maintains the continuity of Nary's story. This is probably the best strategy with younger or less sophisticated readers. Afterward, the story can be reread along with bottom layer, which provides additional information and more context for Nary's story.

STANDARDS: IRA/NCTE Standards 1, 3, 4, 5, 6, 7, 8, 9, 11, and 12; NCSS Standards I, II, III, IV, V, VI, VII, IX, and X

MATERIALS

✔ Knight, M. (1993). *Who Belongs Here? An American Story*. Gardiner, ME: Tilbury House. (one per student)

✔ Anticipation Guide (page 114, one per student)

✔ World Map

FEATURED READING COMPREHENSION STRATEGIES: Anticipation Guide; Text-to-Self Connections

Before Reading

1. Ask students to complete the Anticipation Guide (Readance, Bean, & Baldwin, 1981). Read aloud the eight statements, pausing after each so that students can mark either Agree or Disagree in the columns on the left side of the page. Or, ask students to read the statements and respond to them silently. Collect these papers so that students can refer to them after finishing the book.

2. Then, introduce the book through a class discussion. Start by asking the title question: *Who does belong here? Are all people who live in the United States "Americans"?* Be sure to ask students to explain their reasoning. Record students' answers on chart paper or overhead transparencies for later reference.

During Reading

1. After reading the first page, show students where Cambodia and Thailand are located on a world map. Have students use the illustration on the page to predict Nary's story. As appropriate, provide an update on the relations between the two countries. Individually or in small groups, students may want to do some research on Cambodia. They could visit this Web site and then report their findings to the class: http://www.angkor.ws.

2. For Nary, the abundance of foods is a delight. In the bottom layer of the page with the shopping cart, some of the foods that were brought to the United States are listed. Discuss with students which ones they are familiar with. Ask them what new foods they might add to the list.

After Reading

1. Return the Anticipation Guides to students. Ask them to reread the statements and respond. Ask students to use the book to verify their answers. Then, as a class, document other concepts students have learned about immigration through reading this book.

2. A number of people are mentioned throughout the book, such as Pol Pot, Dith Pran, and Dolores Huerta. Divide the class into small groups and assign one of the people mentioned to each group. Ask students to review what the book said about their assigned person, read the additional information provided in the Notes section in the back of the book, and then search both electronic and print sources for more information. Each group, then, can share their discoveries with the class through a news-show format.

3. On the page about name-calling, the final paragraph asks: "Do you know anyone who is working for change? Are there changes you would like to help make happen? What can you do?" Before talking about the today's world, a class discussion could honor those people students know about who have worked for positive social change—men like Martin Luther King, Jr. and Cesar Chavez and women like Dorothea Dix and Mother Teresa. Then, ask students the questions from that paragraph and urge them to focus on the final question: "What can you do?" Ask students how their answer relates to the title of the book: *Who Belongs Here?*

4. On the last multilayered page, the author writes: "Each of us has stories to tell about our lives, our memories, and our dreams. Sharing our stories, and listening to each other, helps us to understand who we are." Invite each student to write a story about his or her life, a special memory, or dream. When students are finished, invite them to share their stories aloud.

Anticipation Guide

| Before Reading | | | After Reading | |
Agree	Disagree		Agree	Disagree
___	___	1. Immigrants came to America by choice.	___	___
___	___	2. Before people migrated to America, tribes of native people lived here.	___	___
___	___	3. From 1892 to 1954, more than 22 million immigrants from at least 100 countries arrived on boats at Ellis Island.	___	___
___	___	4. Many English-language words come from other languages.	___	___
___	___	5. Peanuts, peppers, corn, and avocados are among America's native foods.	___	___
___	___	6. The goal of the United Farm Workers of America is for all farmworkers to be treated fairly, and to work in a healthy and safe environment.	___	___
___	___	7. Part of the U.S. Constitution was modeled after the Great Law of Peace, a political system that six nations of Iroquois people developed in the 1500s.	___	___
___	___	8. Immigrants to the United States are typically welcomed eagerly and treated well.	___	___

Scholastic Teaching Resources: Teaching Reading Strategies With Literature That Matters to Middle Schoolers 114

TEXT-TO-SELF CONNECTIONS

Extension Activities

- Ask students to pretend that Nary has joined the class. Encourage them to think of ways to make him feel more comfortable. Have them create a list of "Do's and Don'ts." Post these guidelines or create a handout for the class so that they are ready when a new student joins the class.

- Have students find out more about Angel Island and then create a poster sharing what they've learned. Alternatively, students can find out specifically about Chinese immigrants who came through Angel Island by reading oral histories. Students should read through them, choose one, and then pretend to be that person and retell his or her story to the class.

Further Reading

More books by Margy Burns Knight:

Africa Is Not a Country. (2000). Gardiner, ME: Milbrook Press.
Talking Walls. (1995). Gardiner, ME: Tilbury House.
Talking Walls: The Stories Continue. (1997). Gardiner, ME: Tilbury House.
Welcoming Babies. (1998). Gardiner, ME: Tilbury House.

TECHNOLOGY LINKS

For information about Angel Island, visit these sites:

http://www.angelisland.org/
http://www.english.uiuc.edu/maps/poets/a_f/angel/gallery.htm
http://www.angel-island.com (for oral histories)

When Jessie Came Across the Sea

by Amy Hest

Leaving your home, family, and all that is familiar to you requires courage—especially if you are only 13 years old, you are moving a continent away, and you are making the journey alone. So when the rabbi of Jessie's small village announces that he has chosen her to travel to America with the single ticket he has been given, she is sad to leave her grandmother, with whom she lives. But obeying the rabbi's wishes, she reluctantly makes the difficult voyage to America by herself, where she will live with the rabbi's brother's widow and work in her dress shop.

On the crowded ship, Jessie overcomes seasickness and uses her sewing skills to embellish with lace the tattered clothes of several passengers. She also meets kind-hearted Lou, the shoemaker's son, and regrets that she cannot find him as they disembark at Ellis Island. After navigating through customs, a homesick Jessie begins the transition from life in her small European village to living with "Cousin Kay" along the bustling streets of New York City. After three years of sewing, saving the coins she earns, and taking English lessons, Jessie brings her grandmother to the United States—just in time to witness Jessie's marriage to Lou!

One of a growing number of high-quality picture books appropriate for older students, this story serves beautifully as a precursor to longer texts dealing with the topic of immigration. P. J. Lynch's lifelike illustrations add to the emotional impact of a tale that vividly portrays the immigrant experience in America at the turn of the 20th century. Since contemporary adolescents may marvel at Jessie's unquestioning obedience to her elders, a class discussion about cultural expectations and family roles across time is an additional possibility.

STANDARDS: IRA/NCTE Standards 1, 2, 3, 6, 7, 8, 9, 11, and 12; NCSS Standards I, II, and III

MATERIALS

✔ Hest, A. (1997). *When Jessie Came Across the Sea*. Cambridge, MA: Candlewick Press. (one per student)

✔ Sticky-notes

✔ World map

✔ Chart paper and markers

FEATURED READING COMPREHENSION STRATEGIES: Predict; Question; Infer

Before Reading

PREDICT

1. Display P. J. Lynch's striking cover illustration of *When Jessie Came Across the Sea*, obscuring its title with sticky-notes.

2. Explain that this is the front jacket of a book you will be reading aloud, and note the author's and illustrator's names. Challenge students to first examine the illustration carefully. Then they should use the clues it provides to write a title for the story. (If some students are already familiar with the book, request that they refrain from revealing the title just yet. Encourage them to compose alternatives instead.)

KEY BENEFIT
Creating a new title, based only on the cover illustration encourages students to predict and infer words and content in the text, activates background knowledge, and builds anticipation for reading or listening.

3. Break the class into groups of four to share their titles and select their favorite. Record each group's final choice on chart paper and tell them you will come back to this list after the class is finished reading the story.

During Reading

1. Stop intermittently to display illustrations and ask guided questions: *Where do you suspect this village is? Why would the village residents want to leave their homes to live in America? Why do you think the rabbi chose Jessie for this journey?* (Clarify the meanings of *rabbi* and *synagogue* if necessary.) *Notice the illustration depicting living conditions on the boat. Do you suppose these are historically accurate?* Encourage students to raise their own questions

QUESTION

2. Pause at the two-page illustration that is a larger version of the book's cover, encouraging students to orally update their predictions about the book's title. Add to the chart paper list.

3. Finish reading the story, allowing time for more student comments and questions.

After Reading

1. Refer students to the list of titles recorded earlier. Remove the sticky-notes on the book's cover to reveal the actual title. Compare it with the students' list, allowing them to express their opinions about its suitability.

2. Discuss the admittance procedures required of immigrants who entered the country through Ellis Island. Role-play a few of the procedures.

3. Direct students' attention to the following note on the book's copyright page: "The staff of The Jewish Museum in New York City provided generous assistance with this book, checking both the text and the artwork for historical authenticity." Ask what this statement means and discuss why the author might have felt it was important to portray her story as accurately as possible, even though it is fictional. *What research might she have needed to do in order to write this story? What other resources might have been helpful to her?*

INFER

KEY BENEFIT
The ability to infer is an important and frequently underdeveloped comprehension skill. Taking a few minutes to explicitly model and practice how you use visual and print clues to draw inferences is enormously helpful to younger or struggling readers.

4. Revisit the topic of Jessie's native country, which is not identified in the story. Guide students in making inferences: *What country do you think Jessie comes from? What clues in the story or illustrations might give you a hint? What do you already know about immigrants that might help you make a reasonable guess?* If necessary, model by means of a Think Aloud how you would arrive at a conclusion about Jessie's home country. Discuss, for example, Jessie's ethnicity. Help students use information in the story (rabbi, synagogue, and so on) to infer that she is Jewish.

5. Draw students' attention to a large wall map of the world. Ask them to identify the North American and European continents, as well as the Atlantic Ocean, which Jessie crossed in the story. Remind students that, other than Native Americans, *everyone else* came to America from other countries.

Extension Activities

- Students can conduct a "passenger search" on the Ellis Island Web site to discover whether any names of distant relatives appear either on a ship's manifest list or in immigration records.

- In addition to appearing on the cover illustration, the Statue of Liberty is visible on two other pages in *When Jessie Came Across the Sea*. Have students learn more about this important national symbol at the National Park Service's Web site.

Further Reading

Blos, J. (2000). *Brooklyn Doesn't Rhyme*. New York: Aladdin Paperbacks.

Bode, J. (2000). *The Colors of Freedom: Immigrant Stories*. New York: Franklin Watts.

Bode, J. (1995). *New Kids in Town: Oral Histories of Immigrant Teens*. New York: Scholastic.

TECHNOLOGY LINKS

The Louisville *Courier-Journal* Newspaper in Education Web page "Jews in America":
    http://www.courier-journal.com/foryourinfo/120202/120202.html

To conduct passenger searches for immigrants entering Ellis Island, visit:
    http://www.ellisisland.org/search/index.asp?

The National Park Service's Statue of Liberty page:
    http://www.nps.gov/stli/prod02.htm

The Orphan of Ellis Island

by Elvira Woodruff

The Orphan of Ellis Island takes a unique approach to immigration—time travel. At the turn of the 20th century, most immigrants came to America from Europe, through the gateway known as Ellis Island. Such is the case of Dominic. While on a class trip to Ellis Island, he "travels" to Italy in 1908 and after a sojourn and some adventures with three brothers there, "arrives" at Ellis Island. This is a heartwarming story about a contemporary foster child who yearns to find a "real" family and truly belong. This story of three orphans and the need to be connected with others, is told thoughtfully, but not sentimentally.

The impetus for immigration is clear in this text. If the three brothers are to have a chance at a full life, they must travel to the "land of opportunity"—America. Middle graders live this "opportunity" through their education, a concept that may not be apparent to them. This novel invites readers to explore the idea of opportunity and compare their circumstances to the circumstances of the Italian trio and Dominic.

STANDARDS: IRA/NCTE Standards 1, 2, 3, 4, 5, 6, 7, 8, 9, 11, and 12; NCSS Standards I, II, III, IV, V, VI, VII, VIII, IX, and X

MATERIALS

✔ Woodruff, E. (1997). *The Orphan of Ellis Island: A Time-Travel Adventure*. New York: Scholastic. (one per student)

✔ K-W-L chart (page 115, top, one per student)

✔ Woodruff, E. (1999). *The Memory Coat*. New York: Scholastic.

✔ Lawlor, V. (1997). *I Was Dreaming to Come to America: Memories From the Ellis Island Oral History Project*. New York: Penguin.

FEATURED READING COMPREHENSION STRATEGIES: Graphic Organizer: K-W-L Chart; Draw Conclusions

Before Reading

1. Find out what students know about Ellis Island. As a class, begin the K-W-L chart (Ogle, 1986). In the K column, find out what they know—or think they know. Then, complete the W column, what they want to know. List their questions here. Next go to http://www.ellisisland.com with the class and explore the site together. You may want to focus first on the "Tour" section, and then on the "History" section. As questions are answered, fill in the L column, what students learned. This chart can be completed on an overhead transparency, chart paper, or a computer with a projection system.

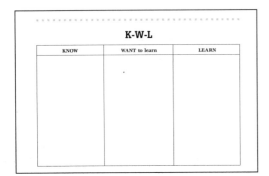

You may also want to contact the education specialist at Ellis Island to borrow the Park in a Pack kit. The kit, recommended for grades 4 through 8, contains a Park in a Pack teaching guide, videos, and many educational activities about the Statue of Liberty and Ellis Island. This traveling educational kit can be borrowed for a period of two weeks. Use of the kit is free of charge, but educators must return it at their own expense, and a deposit is required. For more information, send an e-mail to stli_info@nps.gov.

2. Introduce the book by asking the question: *What is an orphan?* Discuss whether orphans were permitted to enter the United States. Ask students to hypothesize about the main character, Dominic. How might the title connect with his life?

3. Have students take a virtual tour of what it would have been like to arrive at Ellis Island through the eyes of "Mr. Lafata," an immigrant from Italy, at http://www.historychannel.com/ellisisland/index2.html. Continue to add new information to the K-W-L chart.

During Reading

1. After reading the second page, ask students what they know about their "family trees." Once again, students may want to access the official Ellis Island site at http://www.ellisisland.org, this time connecting to the genealogy section. If students know a relative's name, approximately when the relative immigrated, the relative's age at the time, and the point of departure, they may be able to make their own personal connection with immigration through the National Archives and Records Administration. If possible, ask students to create their own family tree.

> **KEY BENEFIT**
> "Technology, integrated into the curriculum for meaningful learning, can be a powerful tool in students' literacy development" (Vacca, Vacca, Gove, Burkey, Lenhard, & McKeon, 2003, p. 340).

2. Dominic thinks frequently about the "perfect" family. Ask students to think about what a "perfect" family would be for them, reminding them it might be the one they have. Ask them to compare their lives with Dominic's. After a class discussion, ask students to write an essay describing a "perfect" family.

After Reading

1. Words of wisdom are interspersed throughout the novel. Ask students to choose one of the following statements, or one that they discover on their own, and comment on it by answering this question: *Why would the statement be appropriate for an immigrant to remember?*

> Coming to a new country is like being adopted into a new family (p. 27).

> All the beauty you could want for a lifetime was in that little village (p. 27).

> Open your heart and all that you need shall be yours (p. 29).

> You know how Father says it takes more strength not to fight than to fight (p. 60).

> But to care about someone else, someone he could lose, was as terrifying to Dominic as it was exciting (p. 67).

2. Read aloud Elvira Woodruff's picture book, *The Memory Coat*. Afterward, ask students to write a similar short story, based on *The Orphan of Ellis Island*. Be sure students have an opportunity to share their work, perhaps on the day they taste biscotti (see the first Extension Activity).

3. The basis for Dominic's "trip" was his listening to one of the 20 voices from the Oral History Library. Read aloud more of these "voices" in *I Was Dreaming to Come to America: Memories From the Ellis Island Oral History Project*. In small groups, students could retell the stories of other immigrants that they choose from the book.

Extension Activities

- To learn about biscotti, students can visit http://www.virtualcities.com/ons/0rec/11biscotti.htm. Invite them to choose a recipe for this Italian cookie, prepare, and then share the biscotti with the class.

- What exactly is a concertina? Students can visit http://www.concertina.info and present what they learn to the class.

Further Reading

Jacobs, W. (1990). *Ellis Island: New Hope in a New Land*. New York: Atheneum.
Levine, E. (1994). *If Your Name Was Changed at Ellis Island*. New York: Scholastic.
Marcovitz, H. (2002). *Ellis Island*. American Symbols and Their Meanings. Broomall, PA: Mason Crest.

Other books about Immigration:
Hoobler, D., & Hoobler, T. (1998). *The Italian American Family Album*. New York: Oxford University Press, Children's Books.
Morreale, B., & Carola, R. (2000). *Italian Americans: The Immigrant Experience*. Immigrant Experience Series. Westport, CT: Hugh Lauter Levin Associates.

TECHNOLOGY LINK

For information about author Elvira Woodruff, visit:
http://www.ewoodruff.com/

In the Year of the Boar and Jackie Robinson

by Bette Bao Lord

It is 1947—in China, the Year of the Boar—and it is the year that Shirley Temple Wong emigrates with her family to Brooklyn, New York, where baseball reigns supreme and Jackie Robinson is its king. For Shirley, it is a learning year—and what Shirley learns through her experiences is, in many respects, similar to what most adolescents eventually learn. Always, however, the daily events of her life in the United States are influenced by the fact that she is clearly "different."

When her father sends word that his wife and daughter are to join him in America, Bandit Wong brightly anticipates that the Year of the Boar will bring "travel, adventure, and double happiness." It brings the expected travel and adventure, but Bandit, whose chosen English name is Shirley Temple, finds that in a foreign culture, acceptance and happiness are hard won. Gamely striving to become an "American," yet understandably missing her home, she learns the true meaning of her grandfather's puzzling saying, "Things are not what they seem. Good can be bad. Bad can be good."

First published in 1984, the story is loosely based on the author's own childhood as a Chinese immigrant in the U.S, and it still has an authentic, contemporary appeal.

STANDARDS: IRA/NCTE Standards 1, 2, 3, 4, 5, 6, 9, 10, 11, and 12; NCSS Standards I, II, III, and IV

MATERIALS

✔ Lord, B. B. (1984). *In the Year of the Boar and Jackie Robinson*. New York: Scholastic. (one per student)

✔ Newspaper photo of naturalization ceremony (transparency) (page 115, bottom)

✔ News article listing names of recently naturalized citizens (one per student)

✔ World Map

✔ Citizenship Test Sample Questions (one per student)

FEATURED READING COMPREHENSION STRATEGIES: Background Knowledge; Visualize; Analyze Figurative Language

Before Reading

BACKGROUND KNOWLEDGE

1. Spend a class session preparing students by activating and building background knowledge about immigrants. Begin by projecting a transparency of the photo of immigrants becoming naturalized citizens. (Cover the photo's caption.) Ask students who they think the people in the photo are, what they might be doing, and why.

2. Discuss and clarify the terms *citizen* and *immigrant*. Ask:

- *In what two ways can people become citizens of the U.S.?*

- *What requirements must an immigrant meet in order to become a naturalized U. S. citizen?*

- *What benefits of citizenship make it desirable?*

If possible, visit the Bureau of Citizenship and Immigration Services' Web site, which defines naturalization and includes FAQs (frequently asked questions) about citizenship.

3. Distribute copies of a news article identifying new U.S. citizens and their countries of origin. (These are regularly published in larger newspapers). Divide students into small groups and instruct them to first read the names of the new citizens. Next they should count the number of countries represented. Then they should tally and/or graph the number of citizens from each country. You might provide a form for this activity with countries listed alphabetically. See the example at right:

4. Use this opportunity to enhance students' geographic literacy: Provide each group of students with a world map or globe and have them locate the countries listed on their tally sheets. Afterward, have them group the countries by continent and rank the continents by the number of immigrants represented. Finally, facilitate a discussion about the results. Ask:

- *Which continent on this particular list has the highest number of immigrants to the U.S?*

- *Which continent was home to the majority of U.S. immigrants in the last century?* (Western Europe)

- *How is the makeup of immigrants in the U.S. changing?* (Most now come from Asia, the Middle East, and the Americas.)

- *How warmly do you think new immigrants are welcomed in this country? Why?*

- *What difficulties might they face?*

- *How might these difficulties be compounded when their native language is not English and their customs and dress are different?*

5. Tell students they are going to be reading a book about a Chinese girl whose family emigrates to the U.S. in the 1940s. Explain that the first chapter takes place in her native country before she leaves for the U.S.

Immigrants at a naturalization ceremony in Boston, where about 3,000 people became citizens on April 11, 2006.

NEW U.S. CITIZENS	
Where from?	How many?
Brazil	1
Canada	2
Germany	1
Guatemala	1
Haiti	1
India	5
Korea	1
Lebanon	1
Pakistan	4
China	2
Philippines	3
Poland	1
Russia	2
Syria	1
Thailand	4
Viet Nam	1

During Reading

1. Though the entire book can easily be read silently, an expressive Read Aloud of Chapter One will facilitate students' appreciation of Shirley's home culture, especially if it's combined with occasional comments and questions. Afterward, ask students to suggest ways in which Shirley's culture is different from that in America (*family roles, respect for elders, holidays, naming traditions, and so on*). In addition, help students observe the similarities between the two cultures: the importance of family, pets, mischievous children, the desire for adventure. Finally, have them consider Shirley's optimism regarding her new home: Ask: *Do you think things will things go as smoothly as she expects? Why or why not?*

VISUALIZE

KEY BENEFIT
Open-Mind Portraits (Tompkins, 1997) promote a richer understanding of a character's psychological evolution. The process engages students, encouraging them to think deeply and reread to validate impressions.

2. The month-by-month arrangement of chapters will help students track the ups and downs of Shirley's life as she adjusts to her first year in America. Have students create Open-Mind Portraits at the end of designated chapters. To create, students should:

   a. Fold a paper in half (or use two separate pages) and draw Shirley's face and features on one side. Label with her name and the chapter title.

   b. On a second side or page, draw the same facial outline, but with Shirley's "mind" open for inspection.

   c. Make sketches in the "open mind" that illustrate Shirley's thoughts. For example, at the end of Chapter One, students may draw members of her family as well as symbols of America to show her mixed feelings about leaving her home. They may also supplement their drawings with relevant words. Share in small groups.

ANALYZE FIGURATIVE LANGUAGE

KEY BENEFIT
This discussion underscores the role figurative language plays in comprehension by helping readers create mental pictures.

3. Investigate the author's use of similes in the story. Instruct students to record at least five similes, along with page numbers in their journals as they read. Examples may include "Mabel shook Shirley like a bottle of catsup"; "the kids who had rallied at Mr. P's disappeared as silently as dandelions in the breeze" (p. 115); and "next year seemed as far away as a balloon lost in summer skies" (p. 147). Afterward, have each student choose at least one simile to illustrate. Share and display them. Discuss the characteristics of a good simile and encourage students to try their hands at weaving similes into their own writing.

After Reading

1. By the time they have read the final chapter, students will have created enough drawings to compile a booklet of the Open-Mind Portraits. This booklet can be a versatile tool for discussion, writing, review, and display. Use the portraits to discuss Shirley's feelings about her new name, getting lost, her first day of school in

America, her teacher, the kids in her class, knowing very little English, not fitting in, her fight with Mabel, and so on. Rich discussions can ensue as students probe the story's events and Shirley's reactions to them.

2. In the June chapter, Shirley blushes, "wishing her teacher would stop praising her, or at least not in front of the others. Already, they called her 'teacher's dog' or 'apple shiner.'" Discuss the meaning of these phrases. Ask:

   • *Why do American students tend to disapprove of "good" students who are well behaved? Is this reasonable or fair?*

   • *What does this say about our views toward adults and education?*

   • *Do you think these same attitudes are prevalent in other cultures?*

3. Later in the same chapter, Shirley's teacher asks: "What is it about baseball that is ideally suited to Americans?" She then launches into a heartfelt patriotic monologue answering her own question. Have students reread this speech and comment on the analogy she makes. Ask:

   • *Is this comparison valid?*

   • *Could you draw a similar comparison between other sports and American citizenship? Why or why not?*

Extension Activities

   • The Dodgers and Jackie Robinson are an integral part of Shirley's life in Brooklyn. Invite students to research the Dodgers and present an interesting fact to the class.

   • Posters of the Dodgers and Jackie Robinson are available to view on the Internet. Students can read a history of the Dodgers ball club and view photos, including several of Jackie in action, stealing home. Search for "Jackie Robinson" or "Brooklyn Dodgers" at www.art.com.

Further Reading

Frosch, M. (1995). *Coming of Age in America: A Multicultural Anthology.* New Press.
Robinson, S. (2001). *Jackie's Nine.* New York: Scholastic.
Yep, L. (1977). *Dragonwings: Golden Mountain Chronicles, 1903.* New York: HarperTrophy.

TECHNOLOGY LINKS

U.S. Citizenship and Immigration Services: http://www.uscis.gov
A Dodgers' history in photos and text:
   http://dodgers.mlb.com/NASApp/mlb/la/history/index

The Circuit: Stories From the Life of a Migrant Child

by Francisco Jiménez

You may have seen and quickly forgotten them: the trucks loaded with laborers en route to or leaving endless fields of cotton, or tomatoes, or strawberries, or grapes, or lettuce, or any of dozens of other farm crops. This autobiographical collection recounts the life of one such family of migrant laborers, the author's family. It began with Jiménez's publication of his acclaimed story "The Circuit," for which the book is fittingly titled. Classified as fiction because the author invented some details to augment his memory of long-past events, the stories are primarily true and wholly unforgettable.

Altogether, 12 short stories make up this memoir. The collection begins with "Under the Wire," in which the author recounts his family's illegal crossing from Mexico to California. From the outset, the Jiménez family's optimism is juxtaposed against the backdrop of the shoddy living conditions they encounter. The quietly determined family follows the migrant circuit from labor camp to labor camp, where they eke out a bare-bones existence. We learn of the events that characterize their lives: the birth of siblings; babysitting mishaps; Christmas gifts; catching fish in mud puddles; foraging through the city dump for furniture and food; the death of a beloved pet; valued possessions; the constant fear of deportation. Jiménez's retellings of his school experiences are especially interesting. Though his education is regularly interrupted by the demands of the migrant life, he does meet some sympathetic teachers and administrators, and he even manages to make a few friends. Two clear themes emerge in the book: (1) Migrant workers are an invaluable and undervalued group in our society, and (2) education is critical. Both are important messages for students, and Jiménez relays them simply and powerfully.

STANDARDS: IRA/NCTE Standards 1, 2, 3, 4, 6, 7, 8, 9, 10, 11, and 12; NCSS Standards I, III, IV, VI, and VII.

MATERIALS

✔ Jimenez, F. (2002). *The Circuit: Stories From the Life of a Migrant Child*. Albuquerque: University of New Mexico Press.

✔ Word Sort Sheet (page 116, one per student)

✔ Scissors (one per student)

✔ Index cards (optional)

FEATURED READING COMPREHENSION STRATEGIES: Prereading Word Sort; Think, Pair, Share; Text-to-Text Connections

Before Reading

1. Distribute Word Sort Sheets and scissors to individuals or pairs of students. The sheets contain 30 words in no particular order: *Guadalajara, California, strawberries, Tent City, jalopy, cotton, tacos, babysitting, furrows, books, Spanish, vineyards, English, tortillas, jacket, camp, Jalisco, notebook, pickup truck, shack, fields, cabin, coffee can, beans, garage, oranges, handkerchief, Fresno, Morelos, green card.*

2. Instruct students to cut the words apart into "cards" and begin sorting them on their desks into groups that contain similarities. You may also want to give students index cards on which they can write other words. Establish a reasonable time limit for the activity.

3. Once students have sorted the words, they should use blank cards to label the categories they have created. Some examples are "Cities," "Vehicles," "Languages," "Buildings," and "Foods." As students think about, discuss, and group the words, they will be developing background knowledge, curiosity, and thinking skills. If they are unable to identify or categorize some words, tell them to create a "Miscellaneous" category, where words can be placed for later exploration. Jalisco and Morelos, both Mexican states, for instance, may not be familiar to students.

4. When time is up, students can meet in groups of four or five to compare categories. Give them a chance to rearrange words if they desire. They should record their lists in their journals. Finally, have the groups report on the categories they have created and explain their reasoning.

5. Tell students you are going to be reading a book of short stories in which they will hear the words they have just categorized. Ask them to hypothesize what the book will be about. Write their predictions on chart paper or the board. Tell them to listen for the words they sorted as you read aloud the story.

Word Sort Sheet				
Guadalajara	California	strawberries	tent city	jalopy
cotton	tacos	babysitting	furrows	books
Spanish	vineyards	English	tortillas	jacket
camp	Jalisco	notebook	pickup truck	shack
fields	cabin	coffee can	beans	garage
oranges	handkerchief	Fresno	Morelos	green card

Scholastic Teaching Resources: Teaching Reading Strategies With Literature That Matters to Middle Schoolers 116

KEY BENEFIT
Prereading word sorts (Hoyt, 2002)—a hands-on activity—prepare students for reading as they activate and "pool" prior knowledge, attend to word meanings and relationships, and develop interest in the topic at hand. Words can also be used later for review purposes.

During and After Reading

1. Read the stories one-by-one on separate days. After each story, have students note the significance of the words that were part of the prereading word sort. Refer to the list of predictions they created. Students should confirm or revise them as needed.

2. Discuss with students the reasons migrant workers are willing to leave their native countries and endure the substandard conditions they encounter here in the U.S. Have them consider the following questions in a Think, Pair, Share format:

- *What impels some Mexicans to risk crossing the U.S. border illegally?*

- *Why do they stay in the United States?*

- *Why do they tolerate long hours, backbreaking work, inferior living conditions, poor pay, and callous treatment?*

- *Does their quality of life really improve? Explain.*

3. Students may be especially interested in the stories of Francisco's schooling and the "English-only" environment he encountered. Ask them to note the coping strategies he used when English was unfamiliar to him, yet he was forbidden to speak his native language. Have students ponder the following:

- *What difficulties do nonnative speakers of English experience in school?*

- *What might the school, the teacher, and students do to help English language learners feel comfortable and participate?*

- *Are there benefits to being bilingual? If so, what are they?*

4. Tell students that the author, Francisco Jiménez, is now a distinguished university professor. Discuss the barriers he likely had to overcome and the persistence he must have demonstrated in order to achieve his goals. Visit Scholastic's Web site to access information about the author. An interview with Jiménez is also available on the site, and students may be interested in reading his responses to questions about both the book and his life.

5. Have students locate quotes from the story that reveal the Jiménez family's attitude toward education. For instance, Mr. Jiménez compliments his son by telling him, "Education pays off. I am proud of you." Discuss with students how a family's views toward education may affect a child's future. Remind them again of the author's success and have them consider how the Jiménez family's emphasis on education might have influenced their son.

6. If your students have read *Esperanza Rising*, compare the two accounts of migrant life. Ask:

- *Do the accounts of migrant life in each book appear to be accurate?*

- *What characteristics of migrant life seem to be constant in both books?*

7. Discuss the book's title. Ask students to consider the meaning of *circuit* and think about how it applies to this story. In what contexts are they familiar with this term? Students should be able to discern that the migrant life is a constant cycle of moving with the seasons and the crops. Moreover, on the book's final page, just as Francisco and his brother are beginning to make progress in their schooling and job situations here in the United States, immigration officials apprehend and deport them. On this level, another circuit has been established: They have come full circle from Mexico to the United States and back again.

Extension Activities

- Amid descriptions of his family's extreme poverty and desperate circumstances, Jiménez also recounts several incidents of kindness shown to him by others. Instruct students to locate and discuss their examples (the conductor of a passing train throws a bag of oranges, apples, and candy to Francisco and his brother; the school principal gives the shivering Francisco a jacket and buys his brother new shoes; the butcher leaves increasingly more meat on the bones Mrs. Jiménez buys for her family meals; a teacher spends his lunch hours teaching Francisco English; a school friend gives him a rare Indian-head penny). Ask students:

  - *What might these actions have meant to Francisco?*

  - *What effect might they have had on the givers?*

- In the book's final story, "Moving Still," the author recalls memorizing the lines of the Declaration of Independence for a school assignment. Visit the <u>American Memory</u> Web site for a lesson plan called "Created Equal?" that focuses on this important concept in the Declaration of Independence.

- If possible, have a bilingual speaker come into the classroom and teach a brief lesson in a language unfamiliar to your students. Follow-up with a discussion about students' feelings and reactions. Relate to Francisco's description of his first experiences as a non-English-speaking student in school.

Further Reading

Cisneros, S. (1991). *The House on Mango Street*. New York: Knopf.

DeFelice, C. (2003). *Under the Same Sky*. New York: Farrar Straus & Giroux.

Hobbs, W. (2006) *Crossing the Wire*. New York: HarperCollins.

Jiménez, F. (2002). *Breaking Through*. New York: Houghton Mifflin. (Award-winning sequel to *The Circuit*.)

TECHNOLOGY LINK

Biographical information and interview with Franciso Jiménez:
   http://books.scholastic.com/teachers/

You can find the "Created Equal?" lesson plan on the <u>American Memory</u> Web site:
   http://lcweb2.loc.gov/ammem/ndlpedu/lessons/01/equal/

Anticipation Guide

Before Reading

Agree   Disagree

After Reading

Agree   Disagree

_____   _____   **1.** Immigrants came to America by choice.   _____   _____

_____   _____   **2.** Before people migrated to America, tribes of native people lived here.   _____   _____

_____   _____   **3.** From 1892 to 1954, more than 22 million immigrants from at least 100 countries arrived on boats at Ellis Island.   _____   _____

_____   _____   **4.** Many English-language words come from other languages.   _____   _____

_____   _____   **5.** Peanuts, peppers, corn, and avocados are among America's native foods.   _____   _____

_____   _____   **6.** The goal of the United Farm Workers of America is for all farmworkers to be treated fairly, and to work in a healthy and safe environment.   _____   _____

_____   _____   **7.** Part of the U.S. Constitution was modeled after the Great Law of Peace, a political system that six nations of Iroquois people developed in the 1500s.   _____   _____

_____   _____   **8.** Immigrants to the United States are typically welcomed eagerly and treated well.   _____   _____

K-W-L

KNOW	WANT to learn	LEARN

Immigrants at a naturalization ceremony in Boston, where about 3,000 people became citizens on April 11, 2006.

Word Sort Sheet

Guadalajara	California	strawberries	tent city	jalopy
cotton	tacos	babysitting	furrows	books
Spanish	vineyards	English	tortillas	jacket
camp	Jalisco	notebook	pickup truck	shack
fields	cabin	coffee can	beans	garage
oranges	handkerchief	Fresno	Morelos	green card

Chapter 6

The Pioneering Spirit

Americans embody the pioneer spirit. After all, our ancestors mustered their resolve, migrated to the shores of this continent, and made their way across its vast expanses to forge new lives. But those settlers in covered wagons are just part of the country's pioneering spirit. People from different eras and of all ages and cultures have been (and are) pioneers. Students are already acquainted with some: Christopher Columbus, Lewis and Clark, and Neil Armstrong, for example. They may realize that Jackie Robinson was also a pioneer as were the Wright brothers and Charles Lindbergh. But others who justly deserve the title may be less familiar to students: Babe Zaharias, the "first lady of twentieth century sports"; Wilma Rudolph, the track star; Ruby Bridges, the first African-American child to attend an all-white school in New Orleans; Sally Ride, the first female astronaut.

Clearly, pioneering involves a lot of "firsts" as J. Patrick Lewis cleverly reminds us in his whimsical poetic tribute, *A Burst of Firsts: Doers, Shakers, and Record Breakers.* Even Elvis qualifies! But pioneering also involves something else: Call it vision, undaunted determination, or the courage to buck tradition and risk it all. No matter. In the end, pioneering means breaking new ground. With that in mind, this chapter invites students to broaden their concept of "pioneers." They will meet an intriguing mix of individuals in this final collection of books.

A Burst of Firsts: Doers, Shakers, and Record Breakers

by J. Patrick Lewis

J. Patrick Lewis's book of verses introduces us to the accomplishments of individuals famous for their achievements. Intermingled with his amusing tributes to playful feats such as the largest bubble-gum bubble ever blown and the first parachute wedding are more-serious poems about some truly remarkable persons: Neil Armstrong, Buzz Aldrin, Muhammad Ali, Ruby Bridges, Toni Morrison, Jackie Robinson, and others. Altogether, 22 poems form this anthology. The author notes beneath each poem's title the subject's name, noteworthy accomplishment, and its historic date. Students will enjoy Lewis's tongue-in-cheek humor while delighting in Brian Ajhar's comic-like illustrations. Witty wordplay combined with factual information about some unforgettable characters makes these verses a good choice for reading aloud in class.

STANDARDS: IRA/NCTE Standards 1, 2, 3, 4, 5, 7, 8, 9, 11, and 12; NCSS Standards I, II, and IV

MATERIALS

✔ Lewis, J. Patrick. (2001). *A Burst of Firsts: Doers, Shakers, and Record Breakers.* New York: Dial Books for Young Readers. (one per student)

✔ Concept Circles #1 and #2 (page 134, one per student)

✔ Dictionary and other reference materials

✔ Chart paper

✔ Computer with Internet access

FEATURED READING COMPREHENSION STRATEGIES: Graphic Organizer: Concept Circle; Set a Purpose; Monitor Comprehension; Analyze Genre

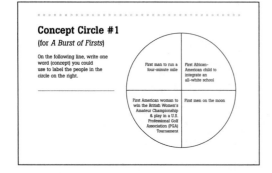

Before Reading

1. Ask students to think of people famous for having been the first to do something noteworthy. If necessary, offer an example. Hold a brief discussion, introducing *A Burst of Firsts* and helping students make the connection between the book's title and its contents.

2. Distribute Concept Circle #1. Tell students to read the "First Person to . . ." example in each of the four quadrants and think of one word that describes or labels them. Scaffold as necessary with prompts such as *What do all these examples have in common? What do we call people who are the first to accomplish great things?* Students can share their ideas with a partner and,

together, select the word they think best represents the concept illustrated, writing it on the line provided.

Discuss as a class, emphasizing the concept of "Pioneers," and telling students you are going to read poems from *A Burst of Firsts* about several people, some of whom are and some of whom are not pioneers. It will be their job to decide.

SET A PURPOSE

During and After Reading

1. Read selected poems that meet your lesson or unit objectives. You may want to begin with the first one, "The Largest Bubble Gum Bubble Ever Blown," since it explains the cover illustration. Continue with other poems that recognize the achievements you wish to highlight, perhaps including "First Child to Integrate an All-White School" and "First Person to Break the Color Barrier in Baseball."

2. Using the *Sports Illustrated* Web site, show students the cover photo of Roger Bannister, the 1954 Sportsman of the Year, and read about this medical student's record-breaking run. Afterward, reread the last few lines of Lewis's poem, "First Man to Run a Four-Minute Mile," beginning with "His body honed to perfect shape."

Discuss Bannister's apparent dedication to his goal, his modesty, and Lewis's description of him as "a boy who chased a dream." Ask: *What does this mean? Is there a difference between "dreaming" and "chasing a dream"?*

3. Next, display the following quote by writer Frank Deford, from a *Sports Illustrated* article dated December 27, 1999:

> "Pioneer miler Roger Bannister and Everest conqueror Edmund Hillary became, at midcentury, the last great heroes in an era of sea change in sport."

If students are to understand the quote, words such as *pioneer, miler, Everest, conqueror, Edmund Hillary, heroes,* and *sea change* invite closer inspection. Encyclopedias and the Internet will provide ready information about Sir Edmund Hillary, the beekeeper from New Zealand who became the first man to reach the summit of Mt. Everest. Use other reference materials to locate, discuss, and illuminate word meanings, guiding students in the process.

MONITOR COMPREHENSION

4. Discuss: *Are all athletes heroes? Pioneers? What exactly is a pioneer?* Collectively compose a definition of *pioneer* as well as the characteristics that distinguish one. Record these on chart paper. Encourage students to think broadly when considering the concept. *Webster's Dictionary*, for example, defines a pioneer as "one who opens up new areas of thought, research, or development." Discuss examples. Post the chart and refer to it throughout your discussions of the poems you read.

5. Before completing the book, have students consider the following: Does being first at something necessarily make someone a pioneer? Encourage them to use the information on the chart they created to review once more the definition and qualities they suggested. Discuss. Finally, distribute Concept Circle #2, a variation on Concept Circle #1. Challenge students to think of three people they consider to

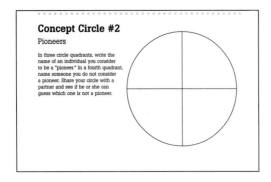

Concept Circle #2
Pioneers

In three circle quadrants, write the name of an individual you consider to be a "pioneer." In a fourth quadrant, name someone you do not consider a pioneer. Share your circle with a partner and see if he or she can guess which one is not a pioneer.

be pioneers and write one name in each three of the circle quadrants. In the fourth quadrant, they should write the name of someone they do not consider a pioneer. Have partners exchange Concept Circles and guess which quadrant contains the name of the "non-pioneer." Discuss.

Extension Activities

- When Roger Bannister was asked to explain what it was that enabled him to break records in running, he replied, "It's the ability to take more out of yourself than you've got." Invite students to consider this quote and its implications. As a whole class activity, locate more quotes offered by record breakers and examine their common themes.

- Bring biographies of other famous people into the classroom. Review the elements of a biography, listing them on chart paper. Ask students to choose any individual they believe is a true pioneer and write a biography about that person, explaining why he or she deserves that designation.

- Many of these poems lend themselves to dramatization. Choose one and reenact it as a class. For example, the action in the poem about Roger Bannister can be replicated outdoors or in a gym. One student can narrate the race (read the poem) as "young Brasher" goes out extremely fast, "Chataway" takes the lead, and Bannister surges forward at the 300-yard mark. A cheering crowd and a timekeeper with a stopwatch will add to the drama of the event.

ANALYZE GENRE

KEY BENEFIT
Reading, discussing, and exploring the features of this literary genre help students more deftly craft their own biographies.

Further Reading

Bannister, R. (1994). *The Four-Minute Mile*. Guilford, CT: The Lyons Press.

Denenberg, B. (1997). *Stealing Home: The Story of Jackie Robinson*. New York: Scholastic.

Freedman, R. (1994). *The Wright Brothers: How They Invented the Airplane*. New York: Holiday House.

Salkeld, A. (2003). *Climbing Everest: Tales of Triumph and Tragedy on the World's Highest Mountain*. Washington, D.C.: National Geographic Society.

TECHNOLOGY LINKS

Sports Illustrated covers and Sportsman of the Year biographies, 1954–present:
http://sportsillustrated.cnn.com/features/2001/sportsman/master_list/
Information about Babe Didrikson Zaharias:
http://sportsillustrated.cnn.com/golf/news/1999/12/02/didrikson_flashback/
Information about Sir Edmund Hillary:
http://www.achievement.org/autodoc/page/hil0pro-1
Sports Illustrated Athlete of the 20th Century nominees and winners:
http://sportsillustrated.cnn.com/features/cover/news/1999/11/03/awards/
http://sportsillustrated.cnn.com/features/cover/news/1999/12/02/awards/

Journey to Nowhere
by Mary Jane Auch

Pioneers of the American frontier endured inhospitable, often harsh conditions in their quest to build new lives. The stories we read, however, are sometimes romanticized versions of their struggles. In this page-turner, Mary Jane Auch gives us a realistic glimpse of the incredible grit it took for pioneers to stay the course.

Neither 11-year-old Mem Nye nor her mother wants to leave their Connecticut farm for the wilds of western New York when her father announces plans to relocate the family. Despite her ardent protests, their cozy farmhouse is quickly exchanged for a covered wagon; Mem's horse, Colonel, gives way to a team of oxen; and with only a few exceptions, the family's prized possessions are sold. With heavy hearts, they say good-bye to family and friends. Only Papa and Mem's 4-year-old brother, Joshua, seem excited about the trip she and her mother call "a journey to nowhere."

Almost from the beginning, disaster plagues the Nyes: Ruffians attack them; Mem is left behind inadvertently and spends a harrowing night in the woods alone; torrential rain muddies roads, swells creeks, and soaks their belongings; wild animals and accidents endanger the family. Throughout the journey, her father is undeterred, her mother is exasperated, her brother is oblivious to the mounting stress, and Mem is clearheaded and plucky.

There is action aplenty in this story, but also warmth and authenticity. Based on actual events the author uncovered through research, the book offers a revealing portrait of 19th-century pioneer life in the eastern United States. With accessible language and a quick-moving plot, it should appeal to a broad range of readers, either as a Read Aloud or independent reading.

STANDARDS: IRA/NCTE Standards 1, 2, 3, 4, 5, 7, 8, 11, and 12; NCSS Standards II, III, IV, and VIII

MATERIALS

✔ Auch, M. J. (1997). *Journey to Nowhere*. New York: Bantam Doubleday Dell Books for Young Readers. (one per student)

✔ Photos of 19th-century farm implements (available on the Internet, large copies for you and several small duplicates to distribute to groups of students)

✔ Data charts (page 135, one per student)

✔ RAFT forms (page 136, one per student)

FEATURED READING COMPREHENSION STRATEGIES: Background Knowledge; Data Chart; Examine Text Features; RAFT

Before Reading

1. Divide the class into small groups and give each a collection of photos of 19th-century farm implements: a plow, a harrow, an auger, a corn planter, or an oxen yoke, for example. Number the photos for easy reference.

BACKGROUND KNOWLEDGE

Data Chart

Item Number	Description	Item Name	Use
1			
2			
3			
4			
5			
6			
7			
8			
9			
10			
11			
12			
13			
14			
15			

KEY BENEFIT

A data chart makes easy work of recording observations in an organized format.

2. Distribute copies of the Data Chart on which students can record their observations about each artifact. Give students five to ten minutes to examine the artifacts in the photos, note their characteristics, and speculate about their uses and names.

3. Groups should share their findings and discuss. Display an enlarged copy of the photos and talk about the objects' names and uses, linking them to the book.

4. Introduce the novel as a pioneer story and instruct students to examine its table of contents. Use chapter titles ("Mountain Screamer," "Snakebite," "The Taste of Dirt," etc.) to inspire interest and generate predictions about plot.

EXAMINE TEXT FEATURES

5. Survey the double-page map that follows the table of contents. Discuss the historical period in which the story takes place and tell students to note the endpoints of the highlighted map route: Hartland, Connecticut, and Sodus Bay, New York. Encourage students to infer which location marks the beginning of the route and which marks its end.

During and After Reading

1. Discuss the possessions and supplies the Nyes took with them on their journey: *Which ones were important for survival? Which ones were important to them for sentimental reasons?* Have students consider which possessions they would take if they were on a comparable journey.

2. Consider how the individual Nye family members—Jeremiah (Mr. Nye), Aurelia (Mrs. Nye), Remembrance (Mem), and Joshua—handled the move. Ask: *Do you suppose it was common for families to have strong feelings about relocating?* Point out Auch's comment in the author's note that discusses this topic.

    Compare the realities of relocating in today's world with those faced by Americans in earlier centuries. Ask:

    • *How important were neighbors and a sense of community to early settlers?*

    • *How important are they to you?*

    • *In what ways were Mem and her family pioneers?*

    • *Could you have done what they did?*

3. In the author's note, Kathryn Auch explains that to tell this story accurately, she had to conduct extensive research. Brainstorm with students a list of the kinds of information she may have needed to find in order to accurately depict pioneer life

in the early 19th century. Discuss how she might have located this information. Then, either take your students to a public library or invite a librarian into the classroom to discuss methods and resources for conducting similar research. With additional help from area historical societies, have students locate and analyze primary-source documents such as letters, journals, photos, and period newspaper articles that illuminate local pioneer history.

4. Instruct students to craft a piece of writing directed to one of the early pioneers they have discovered through their research. Model how to use the RAFT (role, audience, form, and topic) writing strategy (Holston & Santa, 1985).

Steps:

a. Tell students that to show what they have learned through their research, they are to imagine that they could contact one of the pioneers of their community. They should write to one of these early settlers and explain how things have changed since he or she first arrived.

b. Display a RAFT chart and model how to plan the writing assignment. Make notes on the chart as you think aloud:

R = Role:	*I could assume any of several roles—the mayor, a citizen, or a newspaper reporter, for example—but I think I will write as the teacher I am.* (Write "teacher.")
A = Audience:	*I am going to write to _____ , because I found her to be very intriguing when I read about her life. I think she would be truly astonished at what I have to tell her!* (Write the pioneer's name.)
F = Form:	*I think I'll use a letter format to do my writing because it would be informative, yet personal.* Discuss other writing forms such as journal entries, essays, scrapbooks, brochures, etc. (Write "letter" to indicate the form your writing will take.)
T = Topic:	*That's easy. I want to tell _____ about how the town looks now. There's so much to say, though, that it will be hard to limit myself. I think I'll focus on the school: the building, its history, the number of students, the types of classes and materials we have, and the transportation. Wouldn't she be amazed to know that most students ride a bus? Maybe I can even include photos!* (Write "school: physical description, history, students, classes, materials, transportation, photos.")

R·A·F·T Form
(for *Journey to Nowhere*)

R (Role): Who do I want to be when I write?
_____

A (Audience): Who should I write to?
_____

F (Form): What form will my writing take?
_____

T (Topic): What specific topic will I write about, and what supporting information will I offer my reader?

Main topic: _____
Supporting information:
_____
_____
_____
_____
_____

KEY BENEFIT
RAFT helps students conceptualize and organize their writing and *"situates* them in the writing task"—as do all good writing activities (Vacca & Vacca, 2005, p. 384).

c. Distribute RAFT forms to students and give each a chance to plan his or her own writing. Circulate, offering help as needed. (Note: Students should be familiar with the various forms of writing before being expected to use them.) Allow ample class time over several days for students to work on writing assignments. Facilitate the process from the brainstorming through publishing stages. When the projects are completed, share and display them.

Extension Activities

- Ask students to use the Internet to learn about present-day Genesee County, New York, where Mem's family settled more than two hundred years ago. Have them write a letter to Mem about how it has changed.

- Note environmental characteristics of early 19th-century America mentioned in the book. Mem's father, for instance, describes "virgin" and "second-growth" forests. Consider the pioneers' use of resources and their attitudes toward conservation. As a class, make a list of the many ways pioneers used wood to meet their needs. Discuss the need for conservation today as compared with earlier centuries. Might Native Americans have had similar views? How might they have felt about European settlers? Novels such as Elizabeth George Speare's *Sign of the Beaver* shed light on this issue.

Further Reading

Sequels to *Journey to Nowhere*:
Auch, M. J. (2000). *Frozen Summer*. New York: Yearling Books.
Auch, M. J. (2002). *The Road to Home*. New York: Yearling Books.

Other books about early pioneers:
Hermes, P. (2000). *Our Strange New Land, Elizabeth's Diary, Jamestown, Virginia, 1609.* (My America). New York: Scholastic.
Hermes, P. (2001). *The Starving Time. Elizabeth's Diary, Book Two, Jamestown, Virginia, 1609.* (My America). New York: Scholastic.
Holm, Jennifer. (1999). *Our Only May Amelia.* New York: Scholastic.
Speare, E. G. (1994). *The Sign of the Beaver.* New York: Yearling Books.

TECHNOLOGY LINKS
Images of an auger, plow, and yoke can be found at:
http://www.museum.siu.edu/university_museum/museum_classroom_grant/
    Museum_Explorers/school_pages/crossville/tools.htm
For other agricultural implements (corn planter, harrow, plow, and oxen yoke), see Conner Prairie Living History Museum's History Online Web page:
    http://www.connerprairie.org/historyonline/agimp.html
Genesee County, New York, home page: http://www.geneseeny.com/chamber/
Historical information about the town of Williamson and the hamlet of Pultneyville:
http://www.waynecountyny.org/hist_sites/site_list.asp?TownID=14

The Journal of Augustus Pelletier: The Lewis and Clark Expedition, 1804

by Kathryn Lasky

By any measure, Meriwether Lewis and William Clark were considered true American pioneers. However, textbook accounts of their expedition seem dry indeed when compared with the version offered by Gus Pelletier, the fictional narrator of this book, who first shadows, then joins the explorers in their historic adventure.

"The Corps of Discovery: That's what they call this outfit that's going up the Missouri all the way to the sea at the very edge of this continent," explains 14-year-old Gus as he observes the preparations. Commissioned by President Thomas Jefferson to explore the Pacific Northwest, including the newly acquired Louisiana Territory, the group sought a water route that would connect the Atlantic and Pacific Oceans. Persuaded that this legendary Northwest Passage, if found, would serve the young country's economic interests, Congress in 1803 appropriated money for the expedition. Meriwether Lewis, President Jefferson's personal secretary, was the mission's hand-picked leader. He invited his good friend, William Clark, to co-command the incredible 8,000-mile, two-and-a-half-year journey.

In this book, which follows the customary diary format of the popular Dear America/My Name Is America series, Gus gives the reader an up-close-and-personal view of the famed duo. Meanwhile, the reader learns something of the corps' other members: Sergeants Floyd, Gass, and Ordway, and Private Whitehouse—all army volunteers; Clark's slave, York; Sacagawea, her husband, and their infant son, Jean-Baptiste; George Drouillard, the corps' chief scout; and other civilian members. Even Seaman, Lewis's dog, is part of the group. The Native Americans of the Northwest are given credit, too, for their invaluable roles in helping the expedition achieve its goals. They, along with York, Sacagawea, her husband, Toussaint Charbonneau, and Gus, who is "half French and half Omaha Indian," epitomize the diversity that characterizes and enriches our nation.

Through Gus's fictional "observations" of actual events, Lasky fleshes out the expedition's characters, bringing them to life while treating readers to a fascinating dose of history, geography, science, and culture.

STANDARDS: IRA/NCTE Standards 1, 2, 3, 4, 7, 8, 9, 11, and 12; NCSS Standards I, II, III, IV, VII, and VIII

MATERIALS

✔ Lasky, K. (2000). *The Journal of Augustus Pelletier: The Oregon Trail, 1804*. New York: Scholastic. (one per student)

✔ Expedition Members Chart (page 137, one per student)

✔ Maps (copies for students and for display):

  ❏ Louisiana Purchase   ❏ Expedition route and identified U.S. territories—1804

✔ Chart paper

✔ Butcher paper (for time line)

FEATURED READING COMPREHENSION STRATEGIES: Guided Imagery; Graphic Organizer: Chart; Evaluate

Before Reading

GUIDED IMAGERY

1. Use guided imagery to invoke students' involvement in the story. Begin by saying something similar to the following, adding visual and other details as you see fit:

   Imagine you are a 14-year-old boy living in the year 1804. Your mother has died during childbirth, and your stepfather is a cruel, abusive man. You hear of an exciting expedition that is embarking near your town along the Missouri River. Captains Meriwether Lewis and William Clark are directing the mission at the request of President Thomas Jefferson. You don't know these men, but you want to get out of town fast . . . .

2. Display maps that illustrate the expedition's course from St. Louis through the Pacific Northwest, which included territory newly acquired through the Louisiana Purchase. Discuss Jefferson's reasons for promoting the expedition and instruct students to track its progress using Gus's journal entries as a guide. Distribute copies of the maps to students.

3. Have students consider and list the skills that might be needed in an exploration party of this nature (cook, carpenter, hunter, tracker, interpreter, surveyor, naturalist, guide, doctor, cartographer, boatmen, etc.). Distribute a graphic organizer on which students should keep a running list of expedition members as well as the skills and services they provided. (See example at left.) Afterward, discuss what might have happened had the group lacked members with these skills.

Expedition Members Chart

NAME	SKILLS/SERVICES
Meriwether Lewis	Experienced army officer; naturalist; mathematician
William Clark	Experienced army officer; cartographer; negotiator
George Droulliard	Hunter; tracker; scout; interpreter
Toussaint Charbonneau	Interpreter
Sacajawea	Interpreter and liaison with Indian tribes
Sergeant Patrick Gass	Carpenter

Scholastic Teaching Resources: *Teaching Reading Strategies With Literature That Matters to Middle Schoolers 137*

KEY BENEFIT

A completed chart helps students critically assess the contributions of all expedition members—not just its leaders.

During Reading

1. Read the book aloud. Gus's brief journal entries allow for flexibility in terms of breaking up the reading. As an option, you may want to read the book's early pages aloud, then have students read independently.

2. After reading the entry for May 22, 1804, the date the expedition embarked on its journey, have students survey their maps and confer briefly in small groups to predict possible obstacles the party may encounter. For example, the northerly trail hints that climate will be a factor in the group's comfort and speed; the Rocky Mountains will present difficult terrain; rivers may be frozen or dangerous; wild animals may pose a threat. Students should then share their hypotheses with the class as you record them on chart paper. Return to these predictions as the reading proceeds.

3. Students may enjoy creating an illustrated dictionary or field guide of the "new" species of plants and animals these adventurers encountered. (Be sure to show examples of contemporary field guides, as well as those kept during the actual expedition.) If they keep track of them through their readings, students will have a list that includes, among other things, prairie dogs, grizzly bears, badgers, coyotes, the gray wolf, and varieties of spruce, pine, cottonwoods, and yews.

After Reading

1. Have students consider the specific roles that Sacagawea, York, the French, and Native Americans played in the success of the expedition. Make a list of the tribes mentioned in the book and note ways they assisted the explorers. The Shoshone, for example, offered horses for the trek across the Rockies; the Nez Percé taught the group how to eat roots, provided vital information about the rivers ahead, and cared for the expedition's horses; Native Americans guided the party through treacherous river rapids, and much more.

2. Direct students to the Historical Note at the end of the book. Note that once the expedition was completed, Sacagawea and York, Clark's slave, were the only members not compensated for their services. Discuss the equity of this, and the diversity of the people who have made—and continue to make—contributions to this country.

EVALUATE

Extension Activities

- Invite students to compare the Lewis and Clark route with the Oregon Trail. Have the class discuss how they differ geographically and in purpose.

- Examine some of the original journal entries penned by Lewis and Clark and members of their party. As a class, talk about any new information and perspectives the entries add to the book's content.

- Gus elatedly comments in his July 4, 1804, journal entry that the most exciting part of the holiday was the naming of Independence Creek, where they had stopped earlier in the day. "There is something mighty exciting," he adds, "about being part of a group that names things. We are truthfully naming America! That is a powerful notion." Challenge students to research some of the landforms named by the Lewis and Clark Expedition. Talk about the place names in your local area and investigate their origins.

- As a class, construct an expedition time line on butcher paper and display it. Consider whether the expedition achieved its purpose, as well as the ultimate effects of the new information it generated.

Further Reading

DeVoto, B. (1997). *The Journals of Lewis and Clark*. Boston: Mariner Books.

Gass, P., & MacGregor, C. L. (2003). *The Journals of Patrick Gass, Member of the Lewis and Clark Expedition*. Missoula, MT: Mountain Press.

Hunsaker, J. B. (2001). *Sacagawea Speaks: Beyond the Shining Mountains With Lewis and Clark*. Guilford, CT: Falcon Publishing Co.

Philbrick, R. (2001). *The Journal of Douglas Allen Deeds: The Donner Party Expedition, 1846*. (My Name is America). New York: Scholastic.

Stewart, G. W. (1997). *The Pioneers Go West*. New York: Random House.

TECHNOLOGY LINKS

For maps and other information about the expedition, visit these sites:

The expedition route:

http://www.nps.gov/lecl/ppmaps/whistoric%20map%2Ejpg

The Louisiana Purchase:

http://www.nps.gov/lecl/ppmaps/purchase%2Ejpg

Travel map showing the expedition route in sections:

http://staff.washington.edu/~muzi/LC/LCmap.html

Microsoft Encarta (Overview of the Expedition):

http://encarta.msn.com/encnet/refpages/RefArticle.aspx?refid=761569929

National Geographic's Interactive Web site for Kids: "Go West Across America with Lewis and Clark": http://www.nationalgeographic.com/west/main.html

National Geographic Society's Lewis and Clark megasite (journey logs, discoveries, timelines, an interactive map, and more):

http://www.nationalgeographic.com/lewisandclark/

PBS's online Lewis and Clark expedition time line:

http://www.pbs.org/lewisandclark/archive/idx_time.html

PRIMARY SOURCES

Lewis's July 28, 1805, journal entry and sketches regarding the three river forks, as well as a detailed description of Sacagawea's help in the mission:

http://www.mt.net/~rojomo/landc1.htm

The Breadwinner

by Deborah Ellis

Afghanistan, an Asian country half a world away from the United States. What does it mean to be an Afghan child? Is it different from being an American child? How different is life for males and females? Dramatically? Minimally? And how did being an Afghan change in the mid-1990s? For men, women, and children?

The author's note at the end of the novel may be a good place to begin reading, as it contextualizes this timely story. While the story itself is fictionalized, the situation that 11-year-old Parvana and her family face reflects the living conditions for many in contemporary Afghanistan. Whether or not the entire note is shared with the students prior to reading the novel is an instructional choice. The conditions of living, primarily addressed in the last paragraph, may be something that students may be motivated to discover on their own as they read the novel, consistently comparing their own circumstances with Parvana's.

How are Parvana, her mother, and Mrs. Weera "pioneers"? Did they choose to be? Did they have a choice? What lessons can readers learn from this novel?

STANDARDS: IRA/NCTE Standards 1, 3, 4, 5, 6, 9, 10, 11, and 12; NCSS Standards I, II, III, IV, V, VI, IX, and X

> **MATERIALS**
>
> ✔ Ellis, D. (2000). *The Breadwinner*. Toronto: Groundwood Books. (one per student)
>
> ✔ *The Breadwinner* Think Sheet (page 138, one per student)
>
> ✔ Afghanistan Outline Map (page 139, one per student)

FEATURED READING COMPREHENSION STRATEGIES: Quickwrite; Graphic Organizer: Compare/Contrast; Visualize

Before Reading

1. Before beginning this novel, ask each student to make a list of all the things that their status as Americans provides. What freedoms come as a result of their citizenship or residence? Collect these papers so that students can refer to them after finishing the novel. 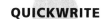 **QUICKWRITE**

2. As a class, ask students to tell what they know about life in Afghanistan. Record their responses on chart paper for future reference. Then, read aloud as much of the author's note at the end of the book as you deem appropriate.

During Reading

1. Read aloud the first chapter. With students, begin making notes on *The Breadwinner* Think Sheet, such as: "Girls were not permitted to go to school. A girl had to cover her head and most of her face with a chador. Women and girls were ordered to stay inside their homes. Women were not allowed to work." As future chapters are read, either aloud or silently, have students continue to add information to the chart. You may want to suggest that students provide page numbers so that they can easily reference their notes.

2. On another sheet of paper, keep track of significant vocabulary words, like *chador*. Help students to define such words using context clues first, and then using the glossary in the book for further clarification.

3. Provide blank maps of Afghanistan. As places are mentioned, ask students to mark the location on their maps.

The Breadwinner Think Sheet

Compare and contrast life in Afghanistan with life in the United States.

LIFE IN AFGHANISTAN	LIFE IN THE UNITED STATES
Girls were not permitted to go to school.	
A girl had to cover her head and most of her face with a chador.	
Women and girls were ordered to stay inside their homes.	
Women were not allowed to work.	

After Reading

1. Parvana says she would like to get a letter. As a way to nurture their own understanding of what it means to "cultivate caring," ask students to write letters to Parvana that would express their concern for her safety and well-being.

> **KEY BENEFIT**
> Reading aloud the initial chapter (or two) of a class novel builds interest and nurtures engagement from the very beginning.

VISUALIZE

2. History was Parvana's favorite subject. Ask students to write a quick paragraph naming their favorite school subject—and why. As students share their responses, create a graph to see which subjects are the most popular.

3. Parvana says to her sister Nooria, "Everybody leans on everybody in this family" (p. 48). Is this a good thing? Why or why not? After students discuss this issue as a class, ask them to write individual position papers.

4. Read aloud the sequels, *Parvana's Journey*, followed by *Mud City*. Then, as a class, discuss Parvana's character. If they deem it appropriate, create a medal for her, along with a proclamation explaining why she is deserving of such an honor.

Extension Activities

- Parvana's father tells her, "Afghans cover the earth like stars cover the sky" (p. 9). Have students research Afghanistan's history and then explain to the class what Parvana's father might have meant by that statement.

- Parvana shares her personal history throughout this book, paralleling it with the political history of her country. As a class, think about how living in America influences our lives, using both the chart paper with the expectations of Afghans and the original lists students wrote before reading the novel. Then ask students to create something such as a poem, a song, an essay, a short story, an editorial, or a poster that celebrates their life in America.

Further Reading

More books by Deborah Ellis:

A Company of Fools. (2002). Markham, Ontario: Fitzhenry & Whiteside.

Mud City. (2004). Toronto: Groundwood Books.

Parvana's Journey. (2002). Toronto: Groundwood Books.

Three Wishes: Palestinian and Israeli Children Speak. (2006). Toronto: Groundwood Books.

For more information about Afghanistan women, try Deborah Ellis' book for adults: *Woman of the Afghan War*. (2000). Westport: Praeger Publishers.

TECHNOLOGY LINKS

For information about author Deborah Ellis, visit these sites:
    http://redcedar.swifty.com/2002/Author_Bios/ellis.htm
    http://www.groundwoodbooks.com/authors/gw_authors.cfm?author_id = 193

Because of the sensitive nature of this topic, these sites are intended for teachers to visit, if interested, for more information about the Taliban:
    http://news.bbc.co.uk/1/hi/world/south_asia/144382.stm

For more information particularly about the Taliban's effect on women, visit:
    http://mosaic.echonyc.com/~onissues/su98goodwin.html

Stargirl

by Jerry Spinelli

The cover of this novel bears only the author's name. The novel's title is only stated symbolically, a yellow star above a green stick-figure girl: Stargirl. In a unit called "Pioneering Spirit," a reader may think that Stargirl is someone from outer space, or perhaps someone far removed from life as we live it. The truth is in the second hypothesis: Stargirl is wholly other-centered. She cares only for the happiness and well-being of others, and not just in her own circle of friends and acquaintances. She cares about the world and each of its inhabitants.

Stargirl is a new student at Mica High School and even by first period on the first day of school of Leo's junior year, Stargirl has created quite a stir. Leo, the narrator of the story, states that she wore "an off-white dress so long it covered her shoes. It had ruffles around the neck and cuffs and looked like it could have been her grandmother's wedding gown. Her hair was the color of sand. It fell to her shoulders. Something was strapped across her back, but it wasn't a book bag. At first I thought it was a miniature guitar. I found out later it was a ukulele" (p. 4). What is even more startling to her fellow classmates than her dress is her actions: She not only played her ukulele in the lunchroom that first day but she sang, "I'm looking over a four-leaf clover that I overlooked before." On another day, she sang "Happy Birthday" to Alan Ferko in the lunchroom, prompting Leo's buddy Kevin to say, "She better be fake . . . If she's real, she's in big trouble. How long do you think somebody who's really like that is going to last around here?" (p. 9).

Leo's thought is "Good question." It is a good question. And it is the heart of this novel. How long can a high school student last if she is kind and good and always looks for the best in others? This is Stargirl's—and Leo's—story, a perfect choice for "Pioneering Spirit." Stargirl's perspective makes her a pioneer of the most central terrain—the heart.

STANDARDS: IRA/NCTE Standards 1, 3, 4, 5, 6, 9, 11, and 12; NCSS Standards IV, V, and X

MATERIALS

✔ Spinelli, Jerry. (2000). *Stargirl*. New York: Random House. (one per student)

✔ The Life and Times of Stargirl Think Sheet (page 140, one per student)

FEATURED READING COMPREHENSION STRATEGIES: Quickwrite; Draw Conclusions

Before Reading

1. Ask students to discuss other books by Jerry Spinelli that they might have read. Ask them to share what they liked best about the books. Ask if any were favorites—and why or why not.

2. With the class, read aloud "Porcupine Necktie," the first two pages of the book. Ask students to predict who sent Leo the necktie for his fourteenth birthday. Record their answers for future reference. Then, ask students what they think Spinelli's purpose was in including these two "preface" pages. Ask how they think this story will link with the rest of the novel. Again, record their answers for future reference.

During Reading

1. Read aloud the first chapter. Discuss the in-school TV show, *Hot Seat*. Ask students to brainstorm who they would interview at their school. In the most positive of ways, encourage students to think of people who are different or interesting.

QUICKWRITE

2. Kevin says Stargirl is "like another species" (p. 32). Archie disagrees. He responds to Kevin, "On the contrary, she is one of us. Most decidedly. She is us more than we are us. She is, I think, who we really are. Or were." In his narration, Leo then says that Archie "talked that way sometimes, in riddles." As a quickwrite, ask students if this is a riddle, or a truth. Ask them how Stargirl could be "more us than we are us," that she is "who we really are." Collect the responses, but discuss them later in the lesson.

3. Stargirl takes Leo to her "enchanted place" and says that in Iceland there are "officially designated 'enchanted places'" (p. 89). When Leo first sees Stargirl's place, he says it "couldn't have been more ordinary," but then he realizes the truth of Stargirl's perspective. Ask students to describe an "enchanted place" they know. Then have students write a letter to the appropriate federal officials, persuading them that the place should have a "stone marker with a brass plate: 'Enchanted Site. U.S. Department of Interior,'" just as Stargirl suggests.

DRAW CONCLUSIONS

4. At one point, Leo tries to explain to Stargirl about the "group thing" (pp. 137–138). With students' copies of the novel closed, read this section aloud—stopping just before the last two paragraphs. Ask them to choose Leo's most compelling argument for conformity. Students will most likely choose, "We live in a world of them, like it or not" (p. 138). Ask students if this rationale is also true for their school. Ask them if it should be. Ask them to predict what Stargirl's reaction will be before reading the conclusion of this chapter.

5. Read aloud the last section of the novel, "More Than Stars." Review "Porcupine Necktie" and students' hypotheses as to its function in the novel. Then, ask students how these two sections function in terms of the whole of the novel, how they serve Spinelli's purpose.

After Reading

1. On page 16, Leo says of Stargirl that he "observed her as if she were a bird in an aviary." Ask students: *If Stargirl were a bird, what kind would she be? Why?* If they can't think of an actual bird she would be, ask them to create a new species that fits her unique nature. Remind them that this new bird would need a name.

2. Have students use the Life and Times of Stargirl Think Sheet to summarize and then graph the events in Stargirl's life. Students should use the numbers along the left-hand side of the grid to gauge the intensity of the event; ten is life at its most stressful. Similarly, have students use the numbers along the bottom as a way to order the events chronologically, writing a brief description in the space provided. Underneath the summary of events, have students hypothesize how many stones Stargirl would have had in her happy wagon at each moment or event. For example, when Stargirl becomes Susan Julia Caraway, dressing just like all the other girls at Mica High, and doesn't get the reception she had hoped for, she has just two stones in her happy wagon (p. 143).

The Life and Times of Stargirl Think Sheet

In the appropriate spaces below, list and summarize the most significant events in Stargirl's life. Next, rate them on the graph—from 1 (ordinary) to 10 (really exciting or stressful). Then, hypothesize how many stones Stargirl would have had in her happy wagon at each of those 10 moments in her life.

3. Archie tells Leo, "Star people are rare. You'll be lucky to meet another" (p. 177). Ask students to consider Archie's assessment of Stargirl. Ask: *Are star people rare? What is a star person? Are we lucky to know them? Is a "star" person always a pioneer? Why or why not?*

Extension Activities

- One of the treasures Stargirl left behind was a homemade photograph album entitled "The Early Life of Peter Sinkowitz." Archie was asked to give it to Peter's parents in five years. It documented special moments in Peter's life. Ask students whose life they would document? Invite them to do so and then give it as a gift.

- As a class, consider starting a club called the Sunflowers—or any other name that honors Stargirl's spirit and philosophy. Write a mission statement and a set of goals for the club that explain that kindness and compassion are at the center of a "pioneering spirit," the heart of humanity.

Further Reading

More books by Jerry Spinelli:
The Night of the Whale. (1985). Boston: Little, Brown.
There's a Girl in My Hammerlock. (1991). New York: Simon & Schuster.
(For additional books, see the bibliography listed with *Maniac Magee* on page 49.)

TECHNOLOGY LINKS

For more information about author Jerry Spinelli, visit
http://www.edupaperback.org/showauth2.cfm?authid=74
For information about creating a kinder world, like Stargirl's, visit:
http://www.actsofkindness.org/

Concept Circle #1

(for *A Burst of Firsts*)

On the following line, write one word (concept) you could use to label the people in the circle on the right.

_____

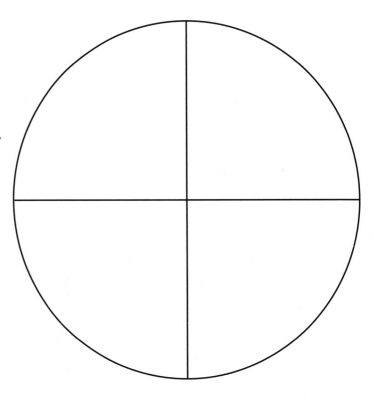

First man to run a four-minute mile

First African-American child to integrate an all-white school

First American woman to win the British Women's Amateur Championship & play in a U.S. Professional Golf Association (PGA) Tournament

First men on the moon

Concept Circle #2

Pioneers

In three circle quadrants, write the name of an individual you consider to be a "pioneer." In a fourth quadrant, name someone you do not consider a pioneer. Share your circle with a partner and see if he or she can guess which one is not a pioneer.

Data Chart

Item Number	Description	Item Name	Use
1			
2			
3			
4			
5			
6			
7			
8			
9			
10			
11			
12			
13			
14			
15			

R·A·F·T Form

(for *Journey to Nowhere*)

R (Role): Who do I want to be when I write?

_____

A (Audience): Who should I write to?

_____

F (Form): What form will my writing take?

_____

T (Topic): What specific topic will I write about, and what supporting information will I offer my reader?

Main topic: _____

Supporting information:

_____

_____

_____

_____

_____

Expedition Members Chart

NAME	SKILLS/SERVICES

The Breadwinner Think Sheet

Compare and contrast life in Afghanistan with life in the United States.

LIFE IN AFGHANISTAN	LIFE IN THE UNITED STATES

Afghanistan Outline Map

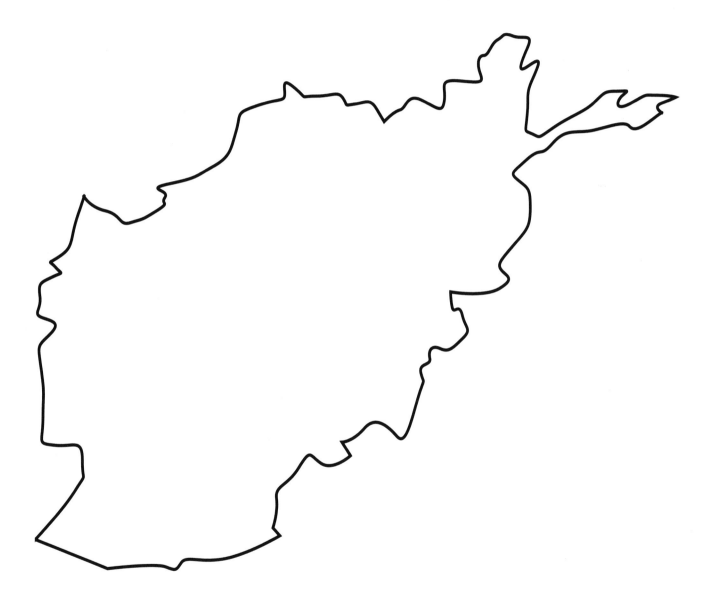

The Life and Times of Stargirl Think Sheet

In the appropriate spaces below, list and summarize the most significant events in Stargirl's life. Next, rate them on the graph—from 1 (ordinary) to 10 (really exciting or stressful). Then, hypothesize how many stones Stargirl would have had in her happy wagon at each of those 10 moments in her life.

Intensity of the Event	1.	2.	3.	4.	5.	6.	7.	8.	9.	10.
10										
9										
8										
7										
6										
5										
4										
3										
2										
1										
Event in Stargirl's Life										
Summary of Event										
Number of Stones in Happy Wagon	___	___	___	___	___	___	___	___	___	___

Appendix

For your convenience, here is information to use when referencing the at-a-glance Standards section included with each lesson.

From the International Reading Association/National Council of Teachers of English Standards for the English Language Arts (1996):

1. Students read a wide range of print and nonprint texts to build an understanding of texts, of themselves, and of the cultures of the United States and the world; to acquire new information; to respond to the needs and demands of society and the workplace; and for personal fulfillment. Among these texts are fiction and nonfiction, classic and contemporary works.

2. Students read a wide range of literature from many periods in many genres to build an understanding of the many dimensions (e.g., philosophical, ethical, aesthetic) of human experience.

3. Students apply a wide range of strategies to comprehend, interpret, evaluate, and appreciate texts. They draw on their prior experience, their interactions with other readers and writers, their knowledge of word meaning and of other texts, their word identification strategies, and their understanding of textual features (e.g., sound-letter correspondence, sentence structure, context, graphics).

4. Students adjust their use of spoken, written, and visual language (e.g., conventions, style, vocabulary) to communicate effectively with a variety of audiences and for different purposes.

5. Students employ a wide range of strategies as they write and use different writing process elements appropriately to communicate with different audiences for a variety of purposes.

6. Students apply knowledge of language structure, language conventions (e.g., spelling and punctuation), media techniques, figurative language, and genre to create, critique, and discuss print and nonprint texts.

7. Students conduct research on issues and interests by generating ideas and questions, and by posing problems. They gather, evaluate, and synthesize data from a variety of sources (e.g., print and nonprint texts, artifacts, people) to communicate their discoveries in ways that suit their purpose and audience.

8. Students use a variety of technological and information resources (e.g., libraries, databases, computer networks, video) to gather and synthesize information and to create and communicate knowledge.

9. Students develop an understanding of and respect for diversity in language use, patterns, and dialects across cultures, ethnic groups, geographic regions, and social roles.

10. Students whose first language is not English make use of their first language to develop competency in the English language arts and to develop understanding of content across the curriculum.

11. Students participate as knowledgeable, reflective, creative, and critical members of a variety of literacy communities.

12. Students use spoken, written, and visual language to accomplish their own purposes (e.g., for learning, enjoyment, persuasion, and the exchange of information).

For more information, visit
www.reading.org/resources/issues/reports/learning_standards.html.

Curriculum Standards for the Social Studies: Ten Themes
(National Council for the Social Studies, 1994):

   I. Culture

  II. Time, Continuity, and Change

 III. People, Places, and Environments

 IV. Individual Development and Identity

  V. Individuals, Groups, and Institutions

 VI. Power, Authority, and Governance

 VII. Production, Distribution, and Consumption

VIII. Science, Technology, and Society

 IX. Global Connections and Interdependence

  X. Civic Ideals and Practices

For more information, visit www.ncss.org.

References

Allington, R. L. (2002). Research on reading/learning disability interventions. In A. L. Farstrup & S. Jay Samuels (Eds.), *What research has to say about reading instruction* (pp. 261–290). Newark, DE: International Reading Association.

Alvermann, D. E. (1991). The discussion web: A graphic aid for learning across the curriculum. *The Reading Teacher, 45,* 92–99.

Alvermann, D. E., & Phelps, S. F. (2005). *Content reading and literacy: Succeeding in today's diverse classrooms.* Boston: Allyn & Bacon.

Atwell, N. (1998). In the middle: *New understandings about writing, reading, and learning.* (2nd ed.). Portsmouth, NH: Heinemann.

Calkins, L. M. (1994). *The art of teaching writing.* (2nd ed.). Portsmouth, NH: Heinemann.

Duke, N. K., & Pearson, P. D. (2002). Effective practices for developing reading comprehension. In A. L. Farstrup & S. Jay Samuels (Eds.), *What research has to say about reading instruction* (pp. 205–242). Newark, DE: International Reading Association.

Elbow, P. (1998). *Writing with power: Techniques for mastering the writing process.* (2nd ed.). New York: Oxford University Press.

Galda, L., & West, J. (1996). Exploring literature through drama. In N. L. Roser & M. G. Martinez (Eds.), *Book talk and beyond. Children and teachers respond to literature* (pp. 183–190). Newark, DE: International Reading Association.

Gardner, H. (1993). *Frames of mind: The theory of multiple intelligences.* (2nd ed.). New York: Basic Books.

Goodman, K. (1986). *What's whole in whole language?* Portsmouth, NH: Heinemann.

Gunning, T. G. (2003). *Building literacy in the content areas.* Boston: Allyn & Bacon.

Guthrie, J. T. (2004). Classroom contexts for engaged reading: An overview. In J. T. Guthrie, A. Wigfield, & K. C. Perencevich, (Eds.), *Motivating reading comprehension: Concept-oriented reading instruction* (pp. 1–24). Mahwah, NJ: Erlbaum.

Hidi, S., & Harackiewicz, J. M. (2000). Motivating the academically unmotivated: A critical issue for the 21st century. *Review of Educational Research, 70,* 151–180.

Hoffman, J. (1992). Critical reading/thinking across the curriculum: Using I-Charts to support learning. *Language Arts, 69,* 120–127.

Holston, J. V., & Santa, C. (1985). RAFT: A method of writing across the curriculum that works. *Journal of Reading, 28,* 456–457.

Hoyt, L. (2002). *Make it real: Strategies for success with informational texts.* Portsmouth, NH: Heinemann.

International Reading Association, & National Council of Teachers of English (1996). *Standards for the English Language Arts.* Urbana, IL: NCTE. Retrieved May 20, 2006, from www.reading.org/resources/issues/reports/learning_standards.html.

Irwin, J. W. (1998). *Reading and the middle school student: Strategies to enhance literacy.* Boston: Allyn & Bacon.

Kasten, W. C., Kristo, J. V., & McClure, A. A. (2005). *Living literature: Using children's literature to support reading and language arts.* Upper Saddle River, NJ: Pearson Merrill Prentice Hall.

Keene, E., & Zimmerman, S. (1997). *Mosaic of thought.* Portsmouth, NH: Heinemann.

Lannen, B. (1999). Cat and mouse. *Mathematics Teaching in the Middle School, 4,* 456-459.

Macon, J., Bewell, D., & Vogt, M. E. (1991). *Responses to literature.* Newark, DE: International Reading Association.

National Board for Professional Teaching Standards (2001). *NBPTS Middle Childhood Generalist Standards* (2nd ed.). Arlington, VA: Author.

National Council for the Social Studies (1994). *Expectations of Excellence: Curriculum Standards for Social Studies, Bulletin 89.* Author.

National Middle School Association (2003). *This we believe: Successful schools for young adolescents.* Westerville, OH: Author.

Ogle, D. M. (1986). K-W-L: A teaching model that develops active reading of expository text. *The Reading Teacher, 39,* 564–571.

Parker, W. C. (2001). *Social studies in elementary education.* (11th ed.). Upper Saddle River, NJ: Merrill Prentice Hall.

Pearson, P. D. (1984). Guided reading: A response to Isabel Beck. In R. C. Anderson, J. Osborn, & R. Tierney (Eds.), *Learning to read in American schools: Basal readers and content texts.* Mahwah, NJ: Erlbaum.

Readance, J., Bean, T., & Baldwin, R. (1981). *Content area reading: An integrated approach.* Dubuque, IA: Kendall/Hunt.

Smith, M. W., & Wilhelm, J. (2006). *Going with the flow: How to engage boys (and girls) in their literacy learning.* Portsmouth, NH: Heinemann.

Tomlinson, C. A. (2003). *Differentiation in practice: A resource guide for differentiating curriculum, grades 5–9.* Alexandria, VA: Association for Supervision and Curriculum Development.

Tompkins, G. E. (1998). *Fifty literacy strategies: Step by step.* Upper Saddle River, NJ: Prentice Hall.

Trelease, J. (2001). *The read-aloud handbook.* (5th ed.). New York: Penguin.

Vacca, J. L., Vacca, R. T., Gove, M. K., Burkey, L., Lenhart, L. A., & McKeon, C. (2003). *Reading and learning to read.* (5th ed.). Boston: Allyn & Bacon.

Vacca, R. T., & Vacca, J. L. (2005). *Content area reading: Literacy and learning across the curriculum.* Boston: Allyn & Bacon.

Vygotsky, L. (1962). *Thought and language.* Cambridge, MA: MIT Press.

Vygotsky, L. (1978). *Mind in society.* Cambridge, MA: Harvard University Press.

Wilhelm, J., & Smith, M. W. (2006). What teachers need to know about motivation. *Voices From the Middle, 13* (4), 29–31.

Wormeli, R. (2003). *Day one and beyond: Practical matters for new middle level teachers.* Portland, ME: Stenhouse Publishers.